Smart
Architecture

Ed van Hinte
Marc Neelen
Jacques Vink
Piet Vollaard

010 Publishers, Rotterdam 2003

The green challenge

We could have been happier, to say the least, five years ago after our search for inspiring examples of green sustainable, ecological architecture. We were dismayed by the pessimism that had in fact marked 'traditional' ecological architecture ever since its emergence in the 1960s. Global disaster was on the way, it proclaimed, thanks to the wastage of fossil fuels and materials and the irreversible pollution of land, air and water. Out of that doom-mongering grew a defensive, conservative architecture with a deep distrust of technological innovation. We could draw little inspiration from this quarter. Surely there had to be an architecture that despite all the major problems brought by our dealings with the environment, was still optimistic? An architecture that would take up the 'green challenge' as the basis for innovation?

We decided to muster this alternative architecture under another slogan: Smart Architecture. Smart, we reasoned, is always good and never pessimistic. Smart is airy and graceful. As a concept it is broader than just sustainability or ecology. Smart architecture obviously is environmentally aware, not just in terms of protecting our environment but because energy and material efficiency is always smart. But there's more to smart architecture than that. It is interactive, a smart building presents itself as an interface between its users and the surroundings. It mediates between the demands and desires of users and environment. In doing so it is behaving intelligently; it uses its sensors to build up a 'memory' and to learn. Smart architecture is efficient, it does more with less. Light and ephemeral may be the most efficient point of departure, or maybe heavy and enduring; it depends on what the use and purpose are. Smart architecture is always time-based, it reacts in differing time cycles to changing user exigencies, climatological conditions, changes of function and social developments. Smart architecture is system-based, it relates back, it is evolutionary, it is network-minded and exhibits swarm behaviour. Smart architecture is 'natural', it speaks for itself, learns from nature, uses it when necessary. Smart architecture sees technology not as an enemy of nature but as a natural ally.

When we looked round again, clutching this new definition, we were all at once confronted with a great many examples of this smart architecture. You can check out the results of our stock-take, begun in 1998, of concepts, designers, techniques and projects on the website www.smartarch.nl. This book is the next phase. In it, three themed chapters based on the key words Time, System and Efficiency, chart the great diversity of departure-points, directions of advancement and concrete answers we encountered. The book ends with a number of examples by architectural practices which, armed with these themes, are blazing new trails in search of a 'green' architecture. Underlying our inventory is the supposition that environmental issues will radically change architecture. The environment is unquestionably one of the key social issues of our day and thus of seminal influence on the course architecture is to take.

It is not so much the built projects, perhaps, that tell us that something has changed fundamentally. Rather, it is the many enthusiastic architects, designers and clients who continue to amaze us with their ideas. This book describes a few of these inspiring projects and thoughts. Not that they are necessarily the best of the batch, an eco-architecture top ten. The many ideas, projects and concepts, large and small, included in these pages are most of all intended as eye-openers and as sources of inspiration. This book asks more questions than it provides answers. We hope it will inspire architects to formulate new questions and new answers and thereby further the cause of a new, smart and vibrant architecture.

Stichting Slimme Architectuur /
Foundation for Smart Architecture

01.
Time
Future dynamics

01.
Future dynamics

If people would waste more time they wouldn't get themselves into so much trouble. The difficulty probably is in determining whether or not time is spent meaningfully, which in turn depends on the definition of time itself. Time is one of those things that everybody intuitively knows the meaning of, but that still is not really understood, not even by physicists. It can be considered some kind of absolute measure that indicates what happens after what, but it is also the opportunity remaining to a person to do all kinds of things before an appointment, and ultimately before he or she dies. Most of what mankind does can be considered to be driven by the fear not to have taken care of everything before the inevitable occurs.

In architecture time usually is a human criterion to describe plans for the building process and what happens thereafter. The community that devotes itself to building is quite good at planning the process. Deadlines are not always met, but by and large buildings are finished within a reasonable time span around the projected date. What happens after that is a different story altogether. Some buildings succeed in surviving generations of people without anyone having arranged this beforehand. Others are demolished way before they were meant to be. It is clear that in this respect time is more often than not overlooked.

The ultimate architectural plan so far has been an illusion. The only successful utopias are the ones in books. Slowly, very slowly, designers are beginning to realize that the future has no final stasis in store for mankind and that people will have to learn to ride the waves of uncertainty. Everything, including ideas about building, will always be changing. This can be taken as a starting point for further development. The efficiency of building functionality needs to increase drastically. It is the human challenge of all times: do more with less. What is meant by 'more' and 'less' needs to be redefined over and over again. In some cases this may lead to flexibility and even throwaway buildings or maybe even degradable cities, in others the message is durability. The common factor is sustainability achieved by tuning quality to the foreseeable future.

In order to find out what has to be done to create this strangely new dynamic efficiency – an open-ended condition to start from rather than a final condition to arrive at – a brief critical description of current Western planning practice is the obvious way to begin. The most important observation is that the planning and design of buildings tends to drift away gradually from actual needs and developments once the building is in place. It usually takes a few years to materialize designs and it is not uncommon for programmatic demands to already begin changing slightly during that period. When a building is finished, different kinds of developments gradually put it under severe functional stress and not just because of the usual mistakes, like hospital beds not fitting through hospital doors. Design constraints for factories, office buildings and schools change every ten years. Office facades are replaced within an average of 20 years. Part of this is due to fashion change. In architecture one could already imagine some 'Style of the Year Award'.
Fashion, however, is hardly recognized as a legitimate parameter by architects, which is strange since architectural style is subject to the same phenomena as fashion, except that its development is one-sided compared to that of clothing because of traditions of style and building. Installations usually have had it after 15 years, with the exception of computer systems that take only a couple of months to become obsolete, if they're lucky. Technological improvements are an important driving force behind aging. A building with up-to-date energy efficiency now, may be hopelessly outdated before you know it. Technology, demographic changes, new commercial opportunities and shifting political opinions are difficult if not im-

possible to predict. It is as if fewer and fewer buildings can cope with that.

The Pantheon in Rome can be a tourist attraction now, even though it started out as a temple in the Roman era and had a church function for quite a few centuries in-between. A modern office building, however, may very well turn into a failure after just a few years, because in hindsight it would have been better if it had been a mix of shops and apartments or had been left unbuilt altogether.

Some building may have been designed as a theatre but has too few restaurants and entertainment facilities in its neighbourhood to be exploited successfully. And in a home the room allocation may suffer in the long run from a wrong estimation. Because of this poor compatibility between plans and changing context, buildings and whole neighbourhoods have to be demolished and replaced before they have had a chance to mature. There is this strange current phenomenon that a building still in use after 50 years, albeit for a purpose different from what it was planned to do, is standing next to one 30 years younger that has to go because this happens to be cheaper than adapting it to new demands. Evidently, something is going wrong in matching design with programmatic constraints. Because of a natural inclination towards efficiency in the limited sense of doing the minimum to comply with the brief, the match between design and programme may become too perfect, leaving no margin for change either, so that it is necessary to completely demolish and rebuild all too soon.

Apparently we still live under the illusion that waste disposal is futile, easy and cheap in relation to the precision with which we can match designs to temporary constraints, either by designing for temporary use, or by incorporating flexibility in the design. Time is hardly a consideration. Things change faster now than ever before, but this doesn't imply that the longer term is obsolescent. We are, however, constantly seduced into frenetic renewal and therefore incapable of thinking ahead of the built result. In addition planning and architecture suffer from a segregation of disciplines, mainly architects, engineers, various suppliers, and builders with different specializations. Together they are trapped in a building tradition in which the lives of buildings after they are finished is simply not an issue.

The alternative, the dynamic condition of sustainability, is by definition generous and forgiving. There are limits to our ability to plan the future. Maybe one third of what is to come can be planned or foreseen, the rest is to remain foggy until further notice. The more we look ahead, the greater the chance that we're wrong. So whatever is projected and built should allow either for easy modification or for a change of programme that implies minimal material adaptation. This begins at the level of city planning, which is dynamic by nature. In this area seduction always works better than force. Even in the virtual city of Alpha World on the Internet participants choose a virtual building location by picking coordinates that are easy to remember. Seduction in its simplest form. Examples from the past further prove this point. The Centre Beaubourg in Paris revived an entire neighbourhood. So if you want certain activities to come alive it is wiser to stimulate and facilitate them than to forcefully allocate them. And when change is called for, it is easier to change the bait than to try and convince the fish. A city is a facility rather than a rigid masterplan, with a given set of buildings and an infrastructure. The more encompassing a plan, the bigger the chance that it, or parts of it, will have the wrong result as time passes.

Architecture and design are always a matter of finding a balance between control and release. But designers of all kinds understandably tend to put the emphasis on the former, because they like to be able to fix and predict the result of their work. They are control freaks, to the point that some won't allow any change to their finished design. This is also a matter of art convention: sometimes the architects who don't mind if their creation crumbles are ignored by the future which judges whether their work has become part of cultural heritage.

More often than not, what happens is control failure. The proof is everywhere. Simple but typical examples are all the walking paths across lawns that originate from people preferring a shortcut to the planned and built road. In the worst cases control failure results in the destruction of costly added value. Because of the observation that a neighbourhood or an office building is surpassed by new demands in a time span as short as 20 or 15 years or even less, added value is tuned to short life spans. In effect this entails a reduction of the quality of use.

The other option is to think in terms of the capacity for adaptation or flexibility. If a reduction of programmed rigidity and thinking in longer terms than just the surrender of finished projects is achieved, then building and sustaining the built environment can become a process that is much more efficient in environmental terms. It becomes generous in the sense that programmes allow for changes of functionality instead of being just a recipe for use, and forgiving in the sense that changes can be made with minimum effort and destruction.

The culture of engineering has turned us into overzealous makers, constantly creating new things to help us save time 'to do something else'. Now it has the opportunity to bring us into the next stage, in which we save time by thinking ahead, constantly reusing what is already there. A major part of what we can reuse, however, still has to be designed. Architectural design can start to incorporate the concept of evolution, creating cities and buildings that intrinsically allow further development without a precise vision of what it is going to be like.

On the one hand it can lead to light and informal city planning with a more flexible infrastructure and greater influence by the inhabitants. Buildings could be recycled after just ten years, or moved to a different spot or just left to nature. Traditionally dwellings are also investment objects. Because of that they are built 'for eternity' as a result of which many houses are no longer in line with current energy efficiency standards.

At the same time the real investment object is not the building but the ground on which it stands. A more intelligent option would be to build light buildings on relatively expensive investment ground. The framework houses of Alsace have been considered moveable for a long time. It is a simple matter of removing the limestone and breaking down the framework to put it up somewhere else. Therefore they are a good example of temporary as well as sustainable architecture. On the other hand there is nothing against buildings that are built to last long, provided they allow different interpretations with regard to functional, technological, economic and cultural evolution.

There are other contextual changes than the programmatic ones, that also can be dealt with in smarter ways. These occur within shorter terms that are defined in length from one year to one day. In fact some of them are closely linked to the very foundation of our chronology. The year of course is a brilliant way to define the change of seasons. Buildings have to be able to protect their inhabitants and users against all the weather's uncomfortable manifestations: cold, heat, rain, wind, snow, you name it. Therefore they must be able to withstand all weather conditions themselves. How complicated this destiny is depends on the climate and their location on the globe. Heating space in the desert requires solutions that differ from those in polar areas. By far the most complicated climate control systems occur in areas with all the extremes of drought and precipitation and heat and cold. It is easier to create an efficient system in the north of Canada, where it is always more or less cold, than in the middle of Russia with icy winters and hot summers. The desert can be both hot and cold, but because temperature variation occurs within a day it is possible to create mutual compensation: use the heat of the day to warm space at night or the other way around.

Computer technology has provided experience in thinking in terms of memory and automatic feed back systems. This gives us the opportunity for a brief side trip to the real-time level that will be dealt with in the chapter on System. Physical phenomena can be exploited in such a way that climate control literally becomes just that: it provides comfort, or heating, or cooling, by letting air and materials do the work through physics instead of turning on a noisy and unhealthy power-devouring climate-conditioning system. Because of the complications mentioned earlier, this becomes more difficult in the face of variations in the weather.

We have now arrived almost automatically at the daily cycle with its most obvious characteristic: night and day. People have become accustomed to the blessings of artificial lighting when darkness rules. This requires a great deal of fumbling around, turning one kind of energy, usually electricity, into light. For it is not yet feasible to store daylight directly for later use. Lighting systems too, however, can be made more efficient. Light can be turned into electricity that can be stored. In addition light allows itself to be reflected and guided to places where it is needed. Some isolated experiments have been going on in this field. There are lamps on the market that work on solar energy. And some large buildings by Norman Foster, Renzo Piano and others possess advanced light reflecting systems. A systematic approach to let lighting control benefit from mass production may lead to drastic improvements.

Use can also be considered a contextual factor for functional properties. It varies with the daily cycle, and with the weekly cycle for that matter.

Functionality can be defined in broader terms than we have become accustomed to. People can sleep in office buildings that are also hotels, and work in sports centres. A great deal of space can be saved if different consecutive activities can take place in the same facility. An office building doesn't have to remain empty during evenings and nights and weekends, and a home garage can be a kindergarten during the day. It is a matter of time awareness and flexible thinking.

Recognition of time with all its nuances instead of just deadlines and eternity can lead to an enrichment of the architectural vocabulary. Accepting the dynamics of buildings and cities, which are now usually ignored or rather considered an unavoidable temporary discomfort, can turn architectural change into an ecologically efficient process as well as a new urban experience.

1.01.
Never-ending
architecture

'If you allow everything and everyone to go their own way you'll end up with chaos.' 'Exactly,' will be Louis Le Roy's reply to the usual criticism of his work, 'that is the whole idea, for only in complex dynamic systems can everything and everybody go their own way. Only in systems like that do I have the guarantee that my freedom is optimized and only then can I go on permanently, exploiting my free creative energy in a continuous flow of time.'

Louis – 'The Wild Gardener' – Le Roy is a Dutch artist, who became well known for his ongoing building and gardening projects. He refuses to even consider the end of the processes he sets in motion. His work consists of trying to free a piece of land in a city and consequently get the neighbourhood inhabitants involved in a continuous process of changing it by building stacks of rubble and seeding plants at will, for years on end. His main enemies are civil servants. They obviously expect some kind of definitive arty creation, but become scared of a loss of control as soon as they begin to realize that there is no end. Le Roy is interested in ongoing processes and a complex entanglement of systems.

His most successful project to date is the Eco-cathedral in Mildam in the north of the Netherlands. At first sight it looks like a neglected forest with a landfill of street rubble. But there is more to it. A closer look shows that there are paths through the wilderness. Between trees and shrubbery you'll find stacked buildings overgrown by vegetation. Louis Le Roy is at work there, has been at work there for 30 years on every day when weather conditions allow it, constantly rearranging pavement tiles, bricks, drains, curbs and all other stony street materials. The stacks, all in balance without any cement, have their own beauty. Le Roy has developed a special skill for this. The paradox is that even though his work looks natural it is man-made. Culture and nature have become one.

Le Roy's work is not, as one might think, naive architecture. He is not making his utopian dream come true. It is the process and its complexity that he is after. He is fighting urban monoculture with vigour. In an article entitled 'Our spectacular society' (1975) he explains his philosophy by strongly criticizing La Grande Borne, an urban planning feat by Emile Aillaud. Despite its many 'cultural' tile tableaux and interesting objects, this neighbourhood is dead. Time is switched off and the inhabitants are not allowed to contribute. In Le Roy's view such a project is doomed, and time has proved that he was right. He based this article mainly on Henri Bergson's 'L'Evolution créatrice', in which the philosopher places man as an active centre in a creative evolutionary process in space and time. Shortlived actions or 'spectacles' can release creative powers for a while, but in the end they have to take place in a time continuum to bring about a true 'évolution créatrice'. Bergson's words are almost literally put into practice by Le Roy. Ironically, it is what mankind does too. It is just that evolution acts up regularly. But the time awareness that Louis Le Roy brings in is quite important. The Eco-cathedral process is due to continue for at least 1000 years.

project: Ecokathedraal
artist: Louis Le Roy
year: 1970-3000
location: Mildam,
the Netherlands

1.02.
Future shrinkage

Architecture can be the beginning of a process rather than the end. That was demonstrated by a multidisciplinary group of four designers working together in Australia. They made a proposal for a limited entry competition to design a university encompassing sustainability in all respects. The commissioning body wanted an entirely different campus concept and that is what they got. It was called 'Future Generations University' and was based on the principle of shrinkage. Only half of the programme was to be built and half of that was planned to dissipate across the world into small auxiliary branches that communicate through the Internet. Instead of being a traditional 'temple of science' this University was to be a forum, where people meet, discuss and learn from each other.

Physically the University is 'lean and clean' and flexible. It consists of two types of buildings. One kind is characterized by 'green membranes', through which it interacts with its environment. These are lightweight structures that can easily be moved and serve to house some 2500 students. The other type has 'information membranes' and facilitates knowledge and argument exchange. These buildings contain work spaces, a conference centre, a library, a theatre and retail facilities and are more definitive in nature. They are placed in the middle of the campus and will continue to function even if the University disappears altogether. The charm of this proposal is that it presents two opposites, the flexible and the fixed, as one.

project: Future Generations University
research and design: Jacques Vink,
Rhea Harbers, Conny Bakker,
Machiel van Dorst and Atze Boerstra
year: 1996
location: Wyong, Australia

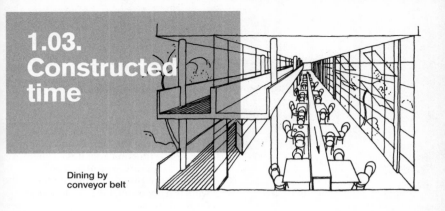

1.03. Constructed time

Dining by conveyor belt

Humanity has somewhat lost the knack of proposing utopias. Times used to be more prosperous for the rigorous rigidity that these ideal organizations entail. The Russian Constructivists in the beginning of the 20th century were still full of hope that they could build a social machine. Their art and architecture, in particular the buildings of Konstantin Melnikov are famous the world over. Less well known is the fact that they didn't just create objects, but that they were trying to determine a social structure to match.

One of the most radical proposals is the plan by Barshch and Vladimirov for a 'Dom Kommuna' or collective condominium. This is one huge building for 1680 inhabitants. It contains as many living cells and extended communal provisions. Families are reduced to their bare essentials: parents or 'productive units', babies, underfives and children of school age. Every category has its own accommodation. The plan is based upon an analysis which was turned into a rigid recipe for all daily life and the entire human life cycle. Most activities, eating, sports, studying, have been scaled up to public urban level. Even the time to take a shower after getting up early in the morning, is prescribed. Everybody, except the youngest age group, consumes food in the same giant restaurant. An inhabitant going into the building will first pass through all the collective facilities. The individual living cell is in the top layer. It is barely comfortable enough to sleep and read a little. The integration of architecture and social structure strongly resembles a beehive. Except that a domkommuna looks better and bees aren't interested in happiness.

project: Dom Kommuna
architect: M. Barshch and V. Vladimirov
year: 1929
location: USSR

Smart architecture is not complicated. Sometimes a simple and hence ostensibly 'dumb' building is smarter than a technology-dominated living-and-working machine over which the user has lost control.

1.04.
Changing
speeds

Buildings aren't just buildings. They can be divided up into seven system-based layers. Each of these has its own lifespan, all the way from centuries down to a couple of years.

1. Location. Generally speaking the geographic location has a very long lifespan. Amsterdam and New York, to name just two examples, have maintained the same grid of streets and roads for many years.

2. Structure. It is quite costly to change the foundation and the main carrying structure of buildings. Therefore their quality determines the architectural endurance of a building. The structure usually lasts between 30 and 300 years.

3. Access. Stairs, escape routes, escalators and lifts have a long life, but not as long as lift shafts that are part of the main structure. Changing these can be a far-reaching process. Emergency and secondary stairs on the other hand may be replaced more quickly because of changing regulations.

4. Facade. If the facade has not been designed to last, it usually has to be replaced or renovated after some 20 years. This is mostly a technical matter but fashion can be a consideration.

5. Services. Systems for climate control, wiring, sprinklers, water and sewers are outdated after seven to fifteen years.

6. Dividing elements. In a commercial context it is common practice to renew doors, inside walls, elevated floors and lowered ceilings as often as every three years.

7. Furniture is replaced fairly quickly.

For a flexible building, by and large, the dynamics of these layers have to be taken into consideration. If, for example, the facade is part of the main structure, the resulting building may be too rigid, because to change the facade the whole building has to be taken apart. The same holds true for a service that is too 'deeply rooted' in the building. Integration of different parts, the destiny of technological development, may hamper flexibility, which is a different kind of development. Like scale (should energy be provided to a city by a power plant or should every building or even every home have its own generator?) flexibility is a complex issue to decide on. Be careful when mixing systems together.

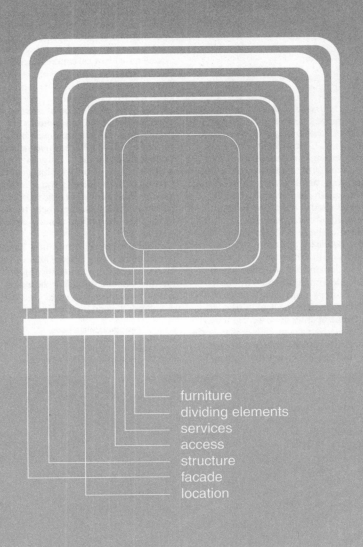

furniture
dividing elements
services
access
structure
facade
location

1.05.
Flexible
concrete

Dealing with change doesn't always have to be designed to work out well. The fact that the Groothandelsgebouw – next to Rotterdam's Central Station – is a well known example of flexibility based on coincidence. One could say that because of its properties it was able to evolve into a structure that is now continuously being adapted to meet new demands. The building can handle this.

Right after the Second World War trade had to be started again almost from scratch and in Rotterdam there was a serious demand for a building where wholesale companies could be domiciled. Perhaps it was an advantage that it was not known in the beginning what kind of companies these were going to be. It was given a neutral floor plan and a strong structure for storage purposes. The total space is no less than 128,000

m², grouped around three inner courtyards where trucks can makes deliveries or collections. Separate spaces can be used both as offices and as storage facilities, all have identical concrete facade elements. Staircases, entrances and a movie theatre provide architectural accents. Currently the Groothandelsgebouw is used to house a collection of companies, a congress centre and a restaurant. People are even living in some remote corners of it. The inherited over- dimensioning allows for industrial activity and archiving. Parts of the wide hallways that were used for the internal transportation are now incorporated in office spaces. Some of the lift shafts have been transformed to hold modern climate control systems.

Flexibility requires organization. Noisy operations are only allowed after office hours. In general, maintenance in flexible buildings is something that should be dealt with at the design stage. One cannot always depend on coincidence.

project: Groothandelsgebouw
architect: H.A. Maaskant and W. van Tijen
year: 1951
location: Rotterdam, the Netherlands

1.06.
From now to eternity

Life span traditionally is hardly a design parameter. Its essence is that functional, economical and architectural aspects of longevity are carefully attuned. This can lead to temporary structures as well as flexible buildings that can last because of their ability to adapt to changing circumstances. Gerd Wingårdh designed a dwelling block for the Malmö Bo01 Housing Exhibition that is built to last for ever. It consists of sturdy materials and has evolved from proven technology. The apartments are roomy and their architecture is meant to withstand changes in trends.

project: housing Bo01
architect: Gerd Wingårdh
location: Malmö, Sweden
year: 2001

1.07.
Crystal skin

In one of his shows the late Dutch comedian Toon Hermans told a story about a place in France where he used to stay, a small inn: 'As a matter of fact it was so small, that when it rained they had to put it inside.' Buildings with two skins to accommodate climate control are not that uncommon anymore. The way in which those skins are designed can still be a source of pleasant surprise. A building complex to house several companies, appropriately called 'Crystalic' because of the way it looks, has two entirely different outsides, one of which is inside. It could also be considered a building inside a greenhouse, a bit like the French inn. It has efficient climate control of course, but there are other advantages. The inside buildings don't have to be wind- or waterproof. Their structure can be simple enough to be easily adapted to changing demands. There have been large-scale unfeasible plans to put domes over entire cities. The problem that arose was that because of condensation of water in the cool upper part, rain would become an everlasting nuisance. On this modest scale, by contrast buildings within a house function well and may keep on doing so for a long time to come.

project: Crystalic
architect: Gunnar Daan
year: 2002
location: Leeuwarden, the Netherlands

1.08.
Changing
flexibility

From the end of the 1960s until well into the '80s most Dutch family TV programmes were broadcast from 'De Meerpaal' in Dronten, a large hall made of steel with glass facades that was designed as a meeting place for anything: sports events, a weekly market, stage plays, with bowling sometimes taking place at the same time. There are several fixed elements, such as two cinema screens, a theatre and a restaurant. The original building stood for everything that characterizes Dutch post-war architecture: belief in progress, the makable society and modernization.

De Meerpaal embraced flexibility but that very characteristic did not remain the same over the years. In 1988 the building was adapted to new local demands. In 1999 it went through a difficult period, because demolition was regarded as unavoidable by the local authorities. A protest action by the Dutch architecture portal Archi-Ned among others, created new chances. A design study was launched and moving De Meerpaal to a different location came under consideration. The Government Architect became involved and seven architecture studios were invited by the Dronten council to make proposals. The plan by Atelier PRO was chosen in 2000. Two extra theatres are now being built. De Meerpaal will rise from its metaphorical ruins in 2004.

project: de Meerpaal
architect: Frank van Klingeren
year: 1967
location: Dronten, the Netherlands

31

1.09.
Wrong place, wrong time

The future can be cruel. Circumstances and opinions change in unforeseeable ways. Duiker, one of the top Dutch architects in the first half of the 20th century, built beautiful buildings. Being a true functionalist he wanted buildings to be broken down when their job was over. One of his masterpieces, however, sanatorium Zonnestraal in Hilversum designed together with Bijvoet, was not demolished and survived in a bad state. It had ended up on the list of important monuments, but for years it kept crumbling until a group of interested people succeeded in giving it a new destination and having it restored. It will again have a medical function. It was meant to last 40 years but now that period has been rewritten as 'eternity'.

project: sanatorium Zonnestraal
architect: J. Duiker, B. Bijvoet and J.G. Wiebenga
year: 1931
location: Hilversum, the Netherlands

1.10.
Miele space station

Forget grinding and shredding and instead reuse, well, everything really to provide new applications. 2012 Architects built their very own space station from old washing machines, thus extending their lifespan. Not that it floats above the earth, but it is mobile and it provides space. It consists of five 60 centimetre wide modules that can each be carried by two people. The five elements can be mounted on top of a trailer to form a caravan. On location the segments can take various configurations. So far the contraption has taken the guise of an art bar, a terrace and a music shop but it can also be an architects' studio. In the latter case it functions as a laboratory used, for example, to survey ways of exploiting waste flows before, during and after the construction of a new neighbourhood.

In its caravan-like constitution the station is already suitable for functioning as a mobile office, but the pick-up truck that pulls it also carries connecting pieces that enable building a camp of about 20 metres long. The modules contain the utilities: kitchen, shower, electronics and archive, whereas the connections provide the space to live and work in. The station is autonomous too. It can take care of its own energy and water management and has a compost toilet and even a greenhouse.

project: Miele Space Station
architects: Jan Jongert, Denis
Oudendijk and Césare Peeren
year: 2003

1.11.
Rethink recycling

The end of the '60s saw the arrival of a counterculture, mostly in the west of the US. Its protagonists established complete idealist villages with peculiar self-wrought shelters. Many of them took the shape of domes, for in those days Buckminster Fuller was the hero of construction. Cult books – 'Shelter' and 'Domes' – were published on these contraptions, and indeed the dome is popular even in Holland where an environmentalist foundation called 'De Kleine Aarde' (Small Earth) builds its own experimental autarkic version. The standard building material is waste. Designer Victor Papanek, famous for his book 'Design for the Real World', advocates the reuse of waste and simple technology to be applied in Third World countries. The cover of his most famous book shows a radio entirely made out of waste materials.

These days reuse and recycling are accepted strategies. In the case of buildings reuse can work very well if it involves waste from the immediate surroundings, because obviously that minimizes transportation. Recycling is a useful way to cleanse the cycle of production and disposal. But currently it can be considered to be slightly overestimated. It is a relatively simple principle. Therefore one tends to view it as an important contribution to counteract pollution. The disadvantage of recycling, however, is that the value that was created before in useful buildings or products is entirely demolished to be created all over again. Both destroying and reproducing involve effort and consume energy, which can be quite inefficient. Sustaining added value over a long period of time can in many cases be a smart alternative to the shredder.

SHELTER

1.12.
Feed car

The vernacular 'Trabbi', better known as the Trabant, the car with the plastic body that conquered Eastern Germany despite its unhealthy coughing sound, is notorious for its inability to be recycled. It is made of Duraplast, a composite consisting of phenolic resin and cotton.

That problem seems to be solved now. 'Rumour has it that the only way to dispose of the bodies was to grind them up and turn them into pig feed', says a website devoted to the Trabant. Edibility is not such a bad option for recycling.

Smart architecture offers an integral solution to a variety of design challenges: the environmental problem, the optimal use of space and other resources, a functional utilization of materials and technology, and aesthetics.

New College in Oxford, UK, is famous for a story told by Gregory Bateson. Allegedly a college restoration committee recently discovered that oak trees were planted in the forest nearby 350 years ahead of their time, to be able to replace the beams in the main hall's ceiling when they started to suffer from dry rot. Bateson remarked: 'That's the way to run a culture.' It is a truly remarkable story, but the New College's website puts it this way: 'The affair of the oak trees.

This is another hoary tale, which has done the rounds in various guises. The story is that when the college fellows decided to restore the hall roof in 1862, they were wondering where to get the oak for the beams to support it. The college woodsman pointed out that their predecessors had planted acorns in their Buckinghamshire woods in about 1380, so that mature trees would be available when needed for the repair of the buildings.'

This story is an embroidery on the theme of continuity and foresight which, when examined in detail, is nonsense. For one thing, the roof of the hall had already been rebuilt once, by a local builder named James Pears in 1786. He used pitch pine timbers and Westmoreland slate. The hall itself had a plaster ceiling in Pears'

design. Hereford B. George in his book 'New College, 1856-1906' said that it had just enough mouldings to give it the appearance of an inverted tea tray. If the college woodsman had been so free with advice in 1862, why did his predecessor hold his tongue in 1786? More pertinently, the Buckinghamshire woods where the mature oaks were felled did not come into the hands of the college until 1441. The truth is that the oaks came from the college woods in Great Horwood, Akeley and Whaddon Chase, where they had indeed been maturing for several hundred years. Yet, if you think back to a society where hardwood was the principal construction material, it is obvious that some trees in every wood had to be left to grow on, while the others yielded a crop of coppiced poles every 15 years or so.

1.14.
Virtual living

Apart from the energy and material needed to build and use computers, which is a lot really, you won't need anything to create a luxurious home with a pool somewhere on the Internet. Alpha World is a 3D virtual environment that was started as soon as web browsers appeared. It evolved from 'computer ancient' concepts called 'Multi User Dungeons', or 'MUDs', that were (and still are) entirely text oriented net communities. In Alpha World, which has several million inhabitants, everybody can build his or her dream home on a spot that is defined by its X and Y values on the Alpha World map. Because it is easier to remember simple numbers, 'from above' the city looks like a cross. There is still a lot of space available, particularly if you don't mind remembering difficult coordinates.

1.15. Sound building

The little lamb is part of nature as is the ancient oak. So are the gnat that brings malaria, poison ivy, meteorites and earthquakes. Gradually man is learning to deal with the latter to some extent. Systems are being developed to prevent buildings from tumbling down. These bear a remarkable resemblance to noise control. An earthquake is indeed a kind of sound of very low frequency and high amplitude, guided by the earth's crust. Therefore preventing earthquake damage entails insulation, damping and vibration control. In high-rise buildings damping may also serve to compensate for the effects of wind force.

An earthquake, beside vertical vibration, mainly consists of horizontal rotation and translation of the earth's crust. Insulation ideally implies that these movements are not transferred to the building. It is like a magician who quickly draws away the tablecloth from under the arrangement of cutlery, plates and glasses. Everything stays in place because of the inertia of the objects and the smoothness of the tablecloth. Buildings can rest on smooth supports on top of the foundations. When the earth moves the foundations will too, but the building remains in place. A new insulation system has been under investigation but has not been applied yet. It starts from the assumption that at a considerable height above ground level it is more difficult for ground shaken by an earthquake to move the mass of a building. The idea, developed by Prof Teiichi Takahashi, is that the building is hung by its roof structure from a very high column-shaped foundation on which it can slide back and forth.

The simplest principle of damping is to passively absorb a major part of the energy that the 'quake' tries to transfer to the building. This can be achieved with elastic materials, like rubber, or with metal that will undergo plastic deformation. Steel spring absorbers, for instance, are transformed during the movement and have to be replaced afterwards. Lead can also be used. Viscous fluids can dampen movement if they have to be pressed through a narrow opening. Generally the energy of movement is transformed into deformation energy, and heat. Electricity for use after an earthquake would be nice

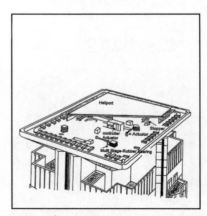

Heliport as mass damper,
Hanku Chayamachi Building,
Osaka, Japan

but is obviously too far away from the concept of disaster prevention to be taken into account.

If the shock energy is forced to move more mass than just the building this has a damping effect too, provided the extra mass is attached to the building as a mass spring system in the sense that it can move relative to the building. The same principle is frequently applied to reduce vibration, even in electric shavers.

All the aforementioned compensation and absorption systems have proved their right to exist but still they are not smart, for their function is not proportional to the earthquake at hand. They are 'passive'. A more refined principle allows adjustment of the mass to tune it to circumstances but the most sophisticated 'active' damping systems work on the basis of direct feedback, which means that they are 'aware' of what they are doing. They react to their own effect by countermovement control of the mass and/or by adjusting the amount of mass involved in the movement, both by means of motors. The 200 metre high building ORC 200 in Osaka, finished in 1993, features two hybrid combinations of passive and active mass dampers on the 51st floor. Rotation is controlled actively and translation passively. They are two concrete blocks of 100 tonnes each on top of layers of rubber. Two motors can adjust the system characteristics by involving less or more of these layers in movement damping. Under normal conditions the blocks are fixed with pneumatic brakes, but if movement exceeds a certain value these are disengaged and the system is 'switched to damping mode'.

Twice 200 tonnes is quite a lot for building elements that enjoy leisure most of the time. An interesting alternative built in the same year in the same city is the Hanku Chayamachi Building, also known as the Applause Tower. The 480-tonne mass on top, which rests on rubber layers and can be moved by two motors, happens to be the heliport. No spare time for this mass.

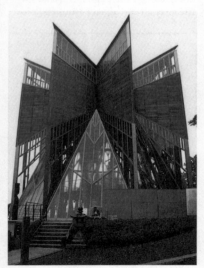

project: Seirei Hall
architect: Shin Takamatsu
year: 1998
location: Mount Myoken, Japan

The building's wooden structure acts as a shock absorber, not only in the event of an earthquake but also to resist the strong winds on the top of Mount Myoken.

1.16.
Sly glass

Climate systems involving glass are not that exceptional anymore. Thomas Herzog, like many an architect, allowed himself to be inspired by the Crystal Palace, the legendary world exhibition building in London, which was built by Paxton in 1851. Herzog's Design Centre in Linz has the same shape of glass roof, but the facade has ventilation valves controlled by an elaborate learning computer system that gets its information from almost 2500 sensors providing feedback to any action that takes place. This system prevents the building from becoming too hot in summer. In addition the roof is kept low to minimize the air volume to be heated. Lighting is also a matter of climate control, especially in the exhibition spaces of a Design Centre. A refined system was developed for tempering the light entering from outside. In the cavity within the double glazing is a micro-mirror screen that transforms the light from unidirectional into diffuse. The screens inside the glass panels have a different direction, depending on the position the panel takes. As a result, seen from the inside the screens facing north are virtually invisible whereas in other directions they give a shimmering impression. An exhibition, even with large objects, looks as though it is in the open air but there are no sharp contrasts.

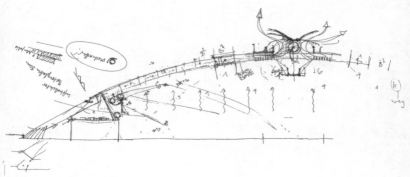

project: Design Center Linz
architect: Thomas Herzog
year: 1993
location: Linz, Austria

02.
System
Cycles and systems

02.
Cycles and systems

In 1859, 24 small systems were brought to Australia. Hobby huntsman Thomas Austin had them sent over from England by his brother. Each consisted of one long-eared furry organism, several dozens pests and any amount of messy microspecies. These systems were called rabbits and they interacted with each other so energetically that only seven years after their introduction 14,253 of them could be shot dead by their only capable enemies: two-legged not very furry small-eared systems armed with rifles. A rifle is a mechanical system capable of firing small lumps of heavy metal at high speed in a certain direction that is then changed by a rather gigantic legless and earless, but nevertheless balanced and rich spherical ecosystem that by and large doesn't do much more than exert gravity and release minute figments of scientific imagination into the universe, occasionally. A visionary called Richard Buckminster Fuller christened this system 'Spaceship Earth', a romantic name since, although Earth moves at high speed relative to fellow celestial bodies, it doesn't really go anywhere interesting. But, like a spaceship containing organisms, it truly is an ecosystem, and a fairly big and vulnerable one too. It consists of numerous interacting sub-ecosystems, one large continent of which was changed dramatically and not very smartly in 1859 by Thomas Austin.

A system is not an objectively observable phenomenon. The word 'system' merely is a means to define a combination of elements that interact with each other and the outside world. Even a layer of paint can be considered a system, and paint marketers don't hesitate to do just that. Systems can clarify architectural planning constraints. They can for instance be defined to achieve input in terms of energy, water, material, information or earthquakes; and because of what all the elements do, they have an output that can consist of waste, products, movement, material and energy, well anything really. To reduce complexity in man-made things like landscapes, cities, buildings, bedrooms and electric tooth brushes, it is quite convenient for the purpose of optimization to define systems and combine these in hierarchies. Something as seemingly simple as a garden shed can be described as a shelter system that protects tools from the rain, and that may have a subsystem to provide electricity and lighting, another for daylight, a closing system that consists of a door with a locking system and a hinging system, but also an ecosystem since it usually is the habitat for a community of spiders, insects, fungus and plants.

In the case of 'ecosystems' the elements always include living organisms and everything they produce, and energy input is required. An ecosystem can be defined as very small, but all the bio-elements inside need to be able to feed on each other. Nowadays you can even buy pocket-size toy ecosystems in glass containers called 'Ecospheres' through the Internet. It is now quickly turning into a successful promotional gift. At the very least an ecosystem with rabbits would need rabbit food that is able to thrive on rabbit excrement, for the interaction between elements always takes the shape of time-consuming cycles in the sense that on the sub-microscopic level atoms and molecules travel around in a circle of consecutive chemical reactions. You can choose any micro-element and observe its adventures of arrival at and departure from different life forms.

An ecosystem usually manifests itself as a balance between plants and animals, bacteria and bacilli and their environment, living on each other's secretions and devouring each other dead or alive, in the meantime getting the benefit of each other's gaseous and liquid by-products. This balance may vary. There is no absolute and objective optimum, although some are more stable than others. A balance that favours one collection of species may be detrimental to another. Species always disappear and evolve and there is a general belief that a wealth of different species is favourable to the success of ecosystems. Like all other organisms people generally prefer ecosystems in which they can survive. For this reason they are now gradually developing a feeling of responsibility to be able to sustain their environment by keeping up the balance to their own advantage.

Cycles in ecosystems can be virtually closed, as in an Ecosphere or a space ship. The only thing that is always needed as an extra is energy. Without that, every ecosystem is doomed. It takes energy to turn chaos into a sophisticated living order.

On a higher level ecosystems interact among themselves, being a part of larger ecosystems. They need to import materials and food and export polluted air and waste. Even earth interacts with other parts of the universe or it wouldn't be hit by meteorites all the time or absorb and radiate heat and light. However, as far as food and materials are concerned, interaction between our planet and our solar system is futile.

Thinking in terms of ecosystems tends to be a bit blurry since it involves life that has a strong tendency to travel. Usually areas that are more or less isolated are defined as ecosystems, but on this planet they are always open to influences from outside such as oil spills, and on the inside changes are going on continuously because of growth, and because of fitter creatures and species surviving at the cost of the less fit.

Cities and buildings can be technically declared ecosystems, although because of their population density they do need food and oxygen from outside and need to get rid of enormous amounts of waste. It is nevertheless quite relevant to consider cities as ecosystems, since they are clearly defined places where different species live and evolve together, influencing one another. Human beings may suffer from the presence of microorganisms and stinging insects, whereas animals and plants, both having to deal with us humans, may have mutual or opposed interests among each other. For a city to be a comfortable habitat, its ecology needs to be healthy. Some circumstances may force inhabitants of large cities, like Mexico City or Athens in Greece, to temporarily close down part of the ecosystem –

car transport, factories – to ensure a healthy environment. Some cities employ biologists to protect the interests of non-human inhabitants.

Eco-buildings may serve to help us understand ecosystems. There have been a few attempts made to build isolated closed environments for a carefully selected combination of species, including humans, to explore the possibilities of creating an ecosystem in space, or on a different planet. Space stations like the former Russian Mir and now the international ISS, and space suits, can be considered quite successful synthetic ecosystems, apart from the fact that astronauts need something to eat along the way. Much more down-to-earth are designs for autarkic houses that ideally don't need any input from central energy and water supplies, nor food input because it would grow on the land around it. Existing natural processes, such as trees taking water from the ground and bugs feeding on leftovers, can help optimize design.

The definition of ecosystems and their often awesome sophistication has proved to be very inspirational. The 'solutions' found in the habitats of groups of plants and animals often are exemplary for ways to optimize cities by trying to mix dwellings and work areas with crop growing facilities, instead of just shops. City Fruitful, a combination of houses and greenhouses, does just that. Buildings can be improved too, with the same principle in mind, and even toys for that matter (Ecosphere). Analysis of the mutual dependence of plants and animals has already taught us quite a lot about survival and needs. Nevertheless we should keep in mind that it provides us with insight into rules and principles: combine animals (including people) and vegetables, keep distances short, try to minimize input and output. This is not the same thing as an ecological appearance with lots of greenery. A striking number of 'environmentally responsible' architectural proposals and realized buildings feature integration of the man-made structure with 'nature', more often than not in the shape of trees. The presence of flowery plants and furry animals may be pleasant, but in itself this is no guarantee for sustainable ecosystem quality. Eco-reality is not as primitive as that. It's the cycle that counts.

Ecosystems have a fairly narrow definition. When we really get into the technicalities of planning and building, the wider notion of system thinking becomes a useful tool. A city can be considered a complicated system in which people live, work, die, have fun or rob banks. It interacts with the surrounding world by absorbing energy, traffic, information and material and disposing of products, waste and other information. The city also interacts with the people using it. The energy subsystem provides electricity, and public space partly serves as a system for information exchange. Traffic systems enable people to move around safely, partly because of the use of the cybernetic principle of feedback: the output of a system is redirected back to the element that controls it. Traditionally the buildings in cities provide people with a comfortable and functional climate. They do so most often by generating it synthetically through a subsystem that consumes energy – often quite a lot of it – and sometimes by interacting with climatic influences.

Some buildings can react to sunlight with shutters or to overheating with valve systems. The feedback principle undoubtedly has the potential to reduce energy consumption, if applied cleverly. This has been done many times already. However, in building there is a tendency to overlook the interrelationship between subsystems and to forget about feedback. It has resulted for instance in oversensitive shutters opening and closing with every passing wisp of cloud because their operation was only linked to incoming light and not to indoor atmospheric conditions.

The rise of computer intelligence may cause a shift in emphasis from synthetic cooling and heating to a more reactive energy household. Buildings as structural systems may be able to react to change by adaptation and self-repair. Connectivity between different systems may lead to one compensating for the failure of another. Systems can be defined on all levels of construction. Wind forces can be counteracted with intelligent sensor-activating contraptions instead of brash oversizing, thereby allowing lighter structures and intelligent ventilation.

Computers are an inspiration for a much broader interpretation of what architecture could be. Buildings that allow easy functional change are an old idea that is now going through a revival that extends as far as creating games and to what is known as kinetic architecture. Architectural systems don't have to be material anymore. It depends on the kind of performance required. They can be interactive systems that react to your every move. However, the promise of computer involvement in living environments is not limitless. Loss of control by over-integration is already emerging, expressed in phenomena such as being unable to close the curtains if the door is still open. Experiments with 'smart houses' have been going on for at least 20 years. The length of that period might mean that this kind of techno-smartness is unwanted.

2.01.
Small worlds
CCCP

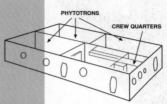

PHYTOTRONS

CREW QUARTERS

In business related to space travel and planet colonization the Russians have proved to be the great initiators. They were the first to experiment with hermetically closed ecosystems, with humans inside them, to find out if we could survive together with a selection of plants without introducing additional food. As early as 1965 in the Siberian town of Krasnoyarsk, they built the Bios-1, a tiny (only 12 m³) 'living' room connected to a tank with algae that produced oxygen from the carbon dioxide exhaled by the one person inside. A supply of food and water, 80% of human survival needs, had to be brought in. In scientific terms this set-up resulted in '20% closure'. Not a very spectacular achievement, but by expanding the Bios-1 into Bios-2, with a water recycling system, bioscientists succeeded in reaching a closure of over 80% three years later.

Their successor, Bios-3, built in 1972 and still functioning today, provides much more comfort with its 315 m³. It consists of welded steel plates and sits pragmatically underground to accommodate a crew of three people with sleeping rooms, a kitchen, a lavatory, a control room and equipment for processing, purification of excretions, and repair. Half the area is occupied by plants in the so-called 'phytotrons', a word coined by American biologists to rival the physicist 'cyclotron' invention. Regeneration of gases seems well under control. Experiments have shown that the closure percentage appears to be hampered mainly by the edibility of plants. The recycling system needs to be much more refined, maybe with contributions by animals, to become really independent.

2.02.
Small worlds US

Of course the Americans couldn't stay behind in researching closed ecosystems. In the '80s they started to build a much more ambitious (over 1200 m²) airtight biolaboratory in the Arizona desert near Tucson. It was to become the famous Biosphere-2. The name suggests that there is a Mark 1, which happens to be Mother Earth herself. The glass facility contains a small rainforest, a bit of ocean, some desert and agricultural terrain and a human habitat, and apart from a rich flora there are several species of insects from all over the world living inside. Like its Russian predecessor, Biosphere-2 was originally meant to explore extraterrestrial colonization. Indeed, two crews of people lived in there. The first eight 'Biospherians' (four men and four women) lived in the artificial ecosystem for two years, despite the level of oxygen going down after nine months, which was solved, and a lack of produce towards the end of the mission. Next, two women and seven men went in. This time problems of a physical and social nature meant that the mission was aborted after six months. The social nut of any system is a hard one to crack for techno minds.
In 1994 it was decided to no longer use this unique laboratory for this - let's face it – rather naive and arbitrary kind of space travel experimentation, considering the range of circumstances on distant planets, and instead focus on research into the Mother Biosphere-1 herself, encompassing programmes for education and public outreach. The laboratory for instance provides unprecedented opportunities for doing ecosystem research and studying climate change. For this purpose the structure was renovated and modified. Now Biosphere-2, managed by Columbia University, employs some 200 people. Since 1996 over 1200 students from many universities have graduated from its programmes.

NEW!
Biosphere 2
World of Discovery
Under the Glass Tour

Now Available!
Click here for details

2.03.
Ecotoys

Anything we know can be turned into a toy, even an ecosystem.

The EcoSphere® claims to be the first self-containing miniature world. It accommodates real life in a glass sphere (or a pod), and you can buy them on the Internet: 'Inside each EcoSphere are active micro-organisms, bright red shrimp and algae in a clear "soup" of filtered sea water. Because the EcoSphere is a self-sustaining ecosystem, you never have to feed the life within. Simply provide your EcoSphere with a source of indirect natural or artificial light and enjoy this aesthetic blend of art and science, beauty and balance.' Until it dies on you after a couple of years. EcoSphere is probably the first ecosystem that can actually break.

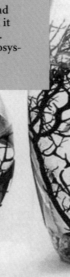

2.04. Cars feed oxygen production

Highways are considered a nuisance that can best be hidden somewhere. On the other hand these functional roads have become familiar in our everyday life and can legitimately be integrated in architectural development. Willemijn Lofvers, Duzan Doepel and Jago van Bergen graduated at the Academy for Architecture in Rotterdam with four ideas that turn the motorway complete with moving vehicles into an integral part of a countryside ecosystem. Here are two: A network of fuel stations branded BP-Koolzaad, accommodates energy vegetation to absorb exhaust gases. Rape, algae, beetroot and willow produce enough fuel for Dutch traffic. The oxygen produced in photosynthesis is used in the combustion process. In this way the fuel station becomes part of the agricultural landscape. Or you could have a Greenhouse Office, a combination of greenhouse landscape and paperwork facilities. All traffic emissions are filtered and fed to the greenhouse plants. Carbon monoxide enriches the soil, small dust particles cleanse the water and the absorption of sulphur dioxide cools the building, providing a comfortable working climate and the recognition that transportation could become part of ecosystem thinking.

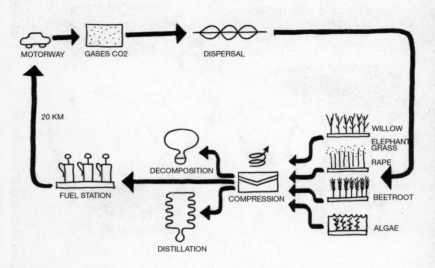

MOTORWAY — GASES CO2 — DISPERSAL — WILLOW — ELEPHANT GRASS — RAPE — BEETROOT — ALGAE — COMPRESSION — DECOMPOSITION — DISTILLATION — FUEL STATION — 20 KM

project: Infra-Ecologie
research and design: Willemijn Lofvers,
Jago van Bergen and Duzan Doepel
year: 1999

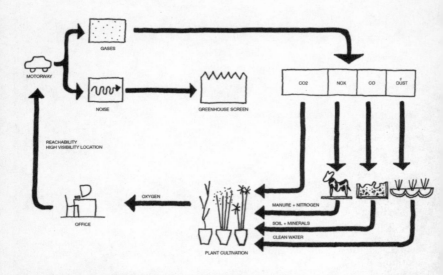

Diagram labels: MOTORWAY, GASES, NOISE, GREENHOUSE SCREEN, CO2, NOX, CO, DUST, REACHABILITY HIGH VISIBILITY LOCATION, OFFICE, OXYGEN, PLANT CULTIVATION, MANURE + NITROGEN, SOIL + MINERALS, CLEAN WATER

2.05.
Industrial ecology

Current industry is caught up in an enormous amount of avoidable wheeling and dealing, for what is waste to one company may very well be raw material to another. So why not put the two close together? Kalundborg in Denmark was the first industrial area to set ecology as a condition for participating industries. An energy producer sells electrical current to a fish breeder, an oil refinery and a plasterboard factory. So far nothing special, but the latter also gets surplus plaster from the energy company's smoke filtering installation. The oil refinery's waste gases go to both the energy guy and the plaster maker and the biotechnological fish

firm sells its nitrogenous deposits to farms in the region. The whole system reduces costs for all parties involved. The principle of this system of 'park management' has three levels. In the first place, cooperation increases eco-efficiency. On top of that, sustainability is enhanced by a more intensive use of space, a shared clean water system and shared environmentally friendly energy resources. The third condition is the forming of an administration to enforce quality standards. Transportation of goods and people and waste disposal can be combined in a synergetic effort.

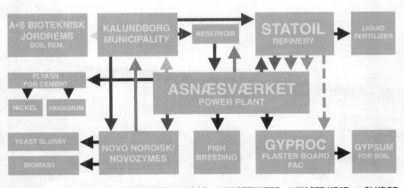

A·S BIOTEKNISK JORDRENS SOIL REM. — KALUNDBORG MUNICIPALITY — RESERVOIR — STATOIL REFINERY — LIQUID FERTILIZER

FLYASH FOR CEMENT — NICKEL — VANADIUM

ASNÆSVÆRKET POWER PLANT

YEAST SLURRY — NOVO NORDISK/NOVOZYMES — FISH BREEDING — GYPROC PLASTER BOARD FAC — GYPSUM FOR SOIL

BIOMASS

■ WATER ■ STEAM ■ COOLINGWATER ■ GAS ■ WASTEWATER ■ WASTE HEAT ■ SLUDGE

Smart architecture is sometimes surprisingly obvious. You get the feeling 'If only I'd thought of that myself'. Simple solutions are anything but dumb. They are beautiful and elegant.

2.06.
Wetland

The more space gets occupied, the more regulations are needed – at least this seems to be the standard opinion in the Netherlands. Currently, guided by a considerable amount of legislation, about a million new dwellings are being built in this country on so-called VINEX locations. In huge projects like this it is difficult to evade regulations, for instance to be able to discover new solutions for housing that don't put too much of a burden on the environment. This is one of the reasons why attempts to create sustainable living conditions are limited to add-ons, like extra insulation and the occasional solar laundry dryer, for houses that may vary in style but all contribute to an extreme suburban monotony.

As it happens, in city planning and architecture many of the aforementioned rules and laws are directly linked to the presence of an infrastructure: water, electricity, gas, sewers and roads. However, regulations simply melt away if the infrastructure is left out. This scheme is used by some designers and architects in the Netherlands to experiment with 'autarkic' housing that is totally independent of infrastructural provisions – almost, that is. Autarkic homes are designed to fit into the local ecosystem on their own terms.

For a competition Tom Mossel, Esther Gonzalez Aurignac and Bert Fraza developed an in some respects less drastic autarkic home as part of a landscaping system called 'Wetland'. In their vision the house is not entirely autonomous: it gets its energy through the mooring post to which it is attached. But it does have a septic tank. Vegetation on the roof purifies grey water and provides insulation. Inhabitants can do their job thanks to the wireless telecommunication network. The house is linked to the existing roads using Stelcon slabs and net reinforced grass in the polder.

The mooring post suggests that the house is a boat, but it is not. The secret is that there are no foundations on heavy and expensive piles that need sinking in a layer of specially raised sand. Instead the principle is applied that an object – in this case a house – can replace a removed quantity of soil with the same weight. Houses will be built on concrete trays. In this way building is possible in marshy areas. Swampy land happens to have been reinstated as normal landscape in large parts of the Netherlands by extending the water buffering zones of the rivers. In this particular project several water levels will occur. In some, the dwellings will start floating every now and then and drift around their poles. These houses will have no fixed orientation or view. Because Wetland has no public space in terms of roads and squares – there are just the concrete slabs and the grass – the allotment will be different, to say the least. The landscape will give an impression of space and be an expression of weather change and flows of water. It all adds up to a system of what could be called 're-pioneering'.

project: Wetland
architects: Tom Mossel, Esther Gonzalez
Aurignac with Bert Fraza
year: 2000
location: the Netherlands

LOW WATER   HIGH WATER   FLOODING

2.07.
Werner Sobek's own house

This professional engineer and architect designed his own perfect dream to live in: Römerstrasse 128. Not only is it designed according to traditional modernist architectural standards in steel and glass, it boasts zero emission and the ability to produce its own heating energy. It has no inside walls, consists of modular elements and functions through the ample application of home electronics with touch screens, voice control and the like, reminiscent of Jacques Tati's 'Mon Oncle'. It can be taken apart and recycled and is lightweight (just under 40 tonnes). On site it leaves a size zero environmental footprint because of triple glazing, heat accumulation in the ground underneath and a solar cell rooftop to keep the heat pump and ventilation system running. It is an intriguing project because of its stubborn combination of environmental awareness and a supposedly correct architectural style.

project: R128
architect and engineer: Werner Sobek
year: 2000
location: Stuttgart, Germany

2.08. Energy labyrinth

The centre of Melbourne recently gained a new space for urban interactivity and cultural opportunities on Federation Square. It is a spectacular atrium, an enclosed street with shops, the National Gallery of Victoria, and room for concerts and performances with glass internally and externally. At the north entrance the space between the glass is extended into an airlock, to prevent warm air from dissipating on cool days. What's more, the building has a unique passive cooling system. The principle is almost as old as civilization, but the Melbourne version is up to date.

Underneath the atrium's structure, and above the deck that covers the railway on the south side along the Yarra River is a dark and complex space called 'the Labyrinth'. Its sole purpose is to accumulate heat. It consists of corrugated concrete walls that additionally support the deck of the square, arranged in cells that together take up a surface of 1600 m². This space would have been useless if the idea had not arisen of storing energy in it.

The Labyrinth exploits Melbourne's variation in temperature. During the night cool air is moistened and pumped through its cells, cooling the concrete walls. By day the air is pumped to the atrium via the cells to provide cooling. As a consequence the temperature inside can be as much as 12°C lower than outside. The cells are not used up all at once. On hot days a portion of them can be held back to be deployed in the evening. In winter, the Labyrinth stores supplemental heat. When the Labyrinth's function is not required for the atrium its cooling capacity is used to pre-cool air for the airconditioning systems of three nearby facilities. The energy system requires only about one tenth of a conventional airconditioning system. CO_2 emission is reduced by the same proportion.

LABYRINTH VENTILATION

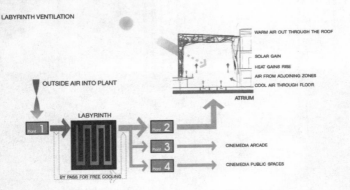

OUTSIDE AIR INTO PLANT

Plant 1

LABYRINTH

BY PASS FOR FREE COOLING

Plant 2
Plant 3
Plant 4

WARM AIR OUT THROUGH THE ROOF
SOLAR GAIN
HEAT GAINS RISE
AIR FROM ADJOINING ZONES
COOL AIR THROUGH FLOOR

ATRIUM

CINEMEDIA ARCADE

CINEMEDIA PUBLIC SPACES

project: Federation Square Labyrinth
and Atrium
architects: Lab Architecture Studio
year: 2000
location: Melbourne, Australia

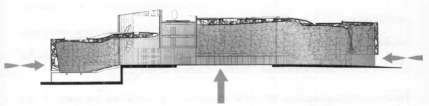

NATURALLY VENTILATED   VENTILATION FROM LABYRINTH   NATURALLY VENTILATED

2.09.
Green stair

The main feature of Mewah Oils Headquarters is a continuous landscaped ramp which links the ground floor all the way up to the roof. Adjoining the landscaped ramp are water features, a grand stair, terraces and a cafeteria. The densely planted landscaped ramp displays a variety of tropical plants while the cascading water feature generates a sonic ambience that relaxes visitors and the building's users alike.

The building almost acts like an organism that hosts people. Like many of Yeang's buildings it has intestines running through it, covered with vegetation. They act like lungs that keep the air clean and moreover guarantee a pleasant space to be and to work in. The plants inside are watered by a system that recycles collected rainwater. Ventilation requires little energy, if any. Nature does the job. In some instances it may get help from electric fans. There is a water feature with cascades that absorb superfluous heat from the air.

project: Mewah Oils Headquarters
architect: Ken Yeang
year: 2003
location: Sengalor, Malaysia

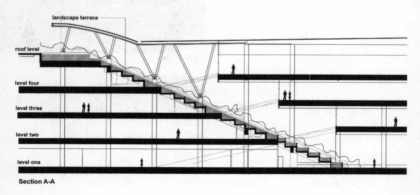

landscape terrace
roof level
level four
level three
level two
level one

Section A-A

2.10.
City Fruitful

Dutch cultivation under glass is huge. It is one of the largest industries in the world. As a consequence, greenhouses - 'the City of Glass' – take up a large area in the west of the Netherlands, land that cannot be used for anything other than harbouring flowers and cucumbers. At the same time this zone is subject to an ongoing urbanization process and is densely populated because of it. Municipalities are almost literally fighting over space for housing. The project 'City Fruitful', planned for an area near Dordrecht, illustrates that there is a lot of space, as well as ecological efficiency, to be gained by radically mixing two purposes. It was done by a group of city planners, architects, market gardeners and technicians. Borderlines between different kinds of use appear to be counter-productive.

City Fruitful is a combination of about 1700 dwellings and 22 hectares of cultivation under glass adding up to 56 hectares altogether. Homes are situated not just next to, but also beneath and on top of greenhouses. Energy, water and waste cycles are closed. Houses will have the same air quality control system as greenhouses, with automatic control of vents and blinds. The roof surface of greenhouses is ideal for passive solar energy generation. Transportation systems are shared between habitation and production. Most of the city,

however, will be car free. There is one main road. Walkers, users of public transportation and cyclists are well off because of the fine-meshed infrastructure. Area use would be about one and a half times greater than in the situation normally prevailing today.

There is also the enhanced quality of both production and living environments. Lastly, the scheme unfolds a new greenhouse typology in which greenhouses can be part private conservatory, part public winter garden.

project: City Fruitful
architects: Kuiper Compagnons,
Kas Oosterhuis Architekten et al.
year: 1992
location: Dordrecht, the Netherlands

2.11.
Scale of limits

Ecology is not as new as it seems. As a discipline it dates from the 19th century. It is rooted in geography and biology, but even though it is as old as many other sciences, it is not a separate university subject. Sybrand Tjallingii is an ecologist and planner. He studied landscape ecology as a part of biology at the University of Utrecht. Later he specialized in landscape architecture and planning at the University of Technology in Delft. At present he is working with the Urban Design and Development Group of the Faculty of Architecture at Delft. The supporting of biodiversity is a paradigm in ecology. There are two viewpoints on which ecological policies rest. The main issue of the theory of 'Island Biogeography' is that of how organisms might reach an isolated habitat, such as an area enclosed by railways. Species will have more difficulty surviving in small and isolated areas. The other is the ecosystem theory: this puts the quality of habitat conditions first. In somewhat exaggerated terms: anything can live anywhere, but the environment selects. Mankind is an integral part of this environment. Sybrand Tjallingii observes that planning decisions reflect mainstream thinking about the relationship between man and nature. Culture and nature are supposed to be opposites. Island thinking rules.

Green borderlines are to separate city and wilderness and designers ban nature from cities, allowing a smattering of lawns at the most. In reality, the limits are not quite that clear-cut. Since 1970 the city has been considered a system, but the question remains of where the borderline should be drawn. There are some in-between solutions now. In Emscher Valley in the west of Germany there has been an attempt to integrate water systems in the city grid by giving the water of the river, which used to be regarded as an obstacle, much more space. The determination of city limits is related to scale. In the early days of environmentalism, when the Club of Rome published its first report, there was a strong tendency towards scale reduction: the world would be better off if everybody were to become a self-supporting farmer. Now ecologists have come to realize that eco-efficiency would perish if that were to happen. Sharing facilities is much more advantageous in urban situations. Compost toilets in a city, for example, are no option. Companies benefit from sharing energy and water facilities. Generally engineers think on a large scale and architects create small-scale solutions. It is quite difficult to make the right choices. Scale and limits are not objectively measurable parameters. They are always subject to decision-making procedures.

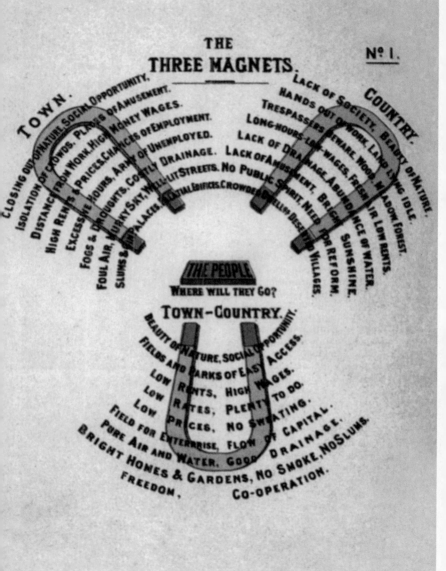

2.12. Water rebalance

'Wrong!', says Dutch landscape architect Dirk Sijmons about the principle of starting a new regional plan by allocating areas to agriculture, offices and homes. 'Water management is paramount in this country, especially in the west.' Indeed it always has been, but because of tradition things are growing out of balance, to the point where floods are bound to occur this century if nothing changes. The water retention capacity of land as it is now is insufficient. The first part of the rationale behind reconsidering the water balance in the west of the Netherlands is that this part has urbanized more than three hundredfold since 1850. Apart from the birth of the so-called 'Randstad', the urban cluster of Amsterdam, Utrecht, Rotterdam, The Hague and everything in-between, this has led to an increase in average soil density and a decrease in open water. The second part of it is land consolidation to increase agricultural productivity. The problem is put on edge as a result of climate change. This is bringing in more and heavier rainfall which also burdens the rivers flowing in from the east through this 'Delta metropolis'.

Sijmons made a proposal for the west of the Netherlands adding extra water retention capacity to the existing system. It consists of peat pasture areas and extra polder drainage areas. In this way the region gets a new system of more sustainable inner lakes that can be financed with private money, simply because people love to live in surroundings like these. Moreover the plan will create recreational opportunities. The planning of buildings will follow suit; some of these will float.

The combination of housing and water retention is worked up in detail for an area near Kamerik, near Amsterdam.

landscape architect:
Dirk Sijmons
year: 2020
location: Randstad,
the Netherlands

75

Smart architecture is optimistic and cheerful and it doesn't have to be expensive. There is always something pleasing about it and often it's even witty. Smart architecture is architecture with a smile – and a sincere one.

2.13. Survival of the cheapest

Julian Vincent is a biomimetics specialist. He works at the Department of Mechanical Engineering of the University of Bath in the UK as a biologist. To illustrate his peculiar job: at some point in the late '90s he was proud to announce that he had been given the opportunity to purchase a penguin to do research to support the development of new insulating materials. Since insulation is relevant to the functionality of building skin here are a few quotes from his analytical descriptions:

'Survival of the cheapest' is Vincent's paraphrase of Darwin's most famous observation. Only the cheapest building design will survive. Vincent refers to energy: 'Organisms have to put a lot of it into keeping a delicate balance between the temperatures inside and outside themselves: under hot conditions one needs to lose heat; when it's cold heat needs to be conserved.' Water plays an important role here, because the best way to lose heat is evaporation. The more 'work' it takes to maintain the right inside temperature the more 'expensive' life gets. The effort is in creating and controlling a rate of temperature change from inside to out. Penguins – here they come – are true masters in this. The gradient can be as steep as 80°C, meaning that such a bird has to be able to maintain a body temperature of about 40°C under polar conditions of minus 40°C. The art lies in having very sophisticated plumage. The down layer close to the body divides the air into parcels. These are so small that the gas becomes more viscous, almost like treacle, and is drastically slowed down because of that: 'We have investigated their feathers. The vane is required simply to provide a smooth and waterproof outer covering. It constitutes only the outer third or so of the feather, the remainder being occupied by long strands of down. We calculated that the average size of air space within the down layer is only about 50 micrometres across. The entrained air can account for the excellent insulating properties of penguin feathers. 'The penguin has a problem, though. When it dives all the air is driven out of the insulating layer by water pressure. If the down were wetted it would lose its ability to subdivide the air into small parcels. So the feathers collapse and lay close to the skin, and have hooks connecting them, rather like Velcro, so that the outer layer remains watertight. When the bird returns to the surface the feathers are pulled back upright, partly by springing, partly by muscles at their base, and the down layer fluffs out again.'

It is a well known fact that penguin feet are not covered with feathers. There is a different principle at work

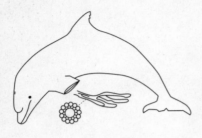

Counter current heat exchange is also to be found in the fins of warm-blooded dolphins.

here: 'counter current heat exchange'. The outgoing arterial blood loses its heat to the venous blood that goes in. This system allows fine-tuned heat regulation. When a penguin emerges its feet are yellow in polar regions but when it waddles ashore on warmer land they are pink, because they are set to get rid of superfluous energy. Counter current heat exchange is not exclusive to penguins or birds. As a matter of fact it is the standard principle in fish and insects, the so-called 'cold-blooded' animals.

Apart from anything else a college room full of students constitutes a room full of small stoves. Temperature control can be a social matter for some species. Vincent: 'A swarm of bees changes its behaviour as the temperature increases. At low temperatures the insects huddle and present a solid shell to the world. The core temperature is 35°C, although the outside of the swarm is colder. At an external temperature of 30°C the swarm seems to have grown due to the incorporation of airways through the middle to convey some of the inside heat away.

Bees overwinter using the design of the nest and stored nectar to maintain viable temperatures. Clustered in the centre of the comb and shivering to produce heat they can easily survive long periods of frost. During summer the nest is cooled by forced evaporation. Bees sit at the front entrance of the hive, which is always at a low position, and fan their wings so that the air is driven through. Water brought into the hive by foraging bees (some of it in the gathered honey) evaporates. Any undesired holes in the outside of the nest are blocked with a waxy material called propolis.' And this is not unlike the application of weather stripping we know from humans.

Summary of a 1998 paper
by Julian Vincent

— stiff, lanceolate main feather
— downy under-feather
highly modified feather

Penguin feather

2.14.
Hot dog
system

System thinking in relation to smart architecture tends to be associated with sensors and computers controlling valves and shutters and lighting, generally things that are dynamic but don't move around. That needn't be so. Australian artist and researcher at MIT media lab Natalie Jeremijenko loves to mix phenomena from different worlds. Her mission is 'to reclaim technology from the idealized, abstract concept of "cyberspace" and apply it to the messy complexities of the real world'. So for instance she reclaims technology from the world of toys in her Feral Robotic Dog project. For the past few years she has hacked several species of toy robotic dogs to do dangerous security jobs. She develops hobby kits to turn robo-dogs into specialized toxin sniffers that wander around in shopping malls and other public facilities to track down poisonous or radioactive substances. The project provides instructions to rebuild your own electronic pet into a well-trained specialist watchdog. One of the models she used is Sony's Aibo. The company protested against this unforeseen exploitation of their carefully developed pet.

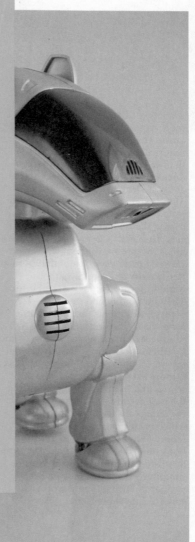

2.15.
Natural models

Rain, heat, distance, gravity, finding food: we humans clearly are champions in adapting to the difficulties that nature presents us with, so much so that we tend to become counterproductive. We owe our resilience to our ability to learn and to understand. Mankind has invented ways to create near-perfect artificial ecosystems and copied the achievements of fellow species. The cliché example is the termite hill, a living environment with an advanced ventilation system that miraculously emerges from the simple behaviour of extremely stupid insects. The functioning and structure of plants and animals themselves also serves as an inspiration, judging by, say, the striking similarity between the 'Mathematical Bridge' at Queen's College in Cambridge and bone structure. A more extreme example is the research that has been going on during the past decade into the workings of the nanoscale 'flagellar motor' by which bacteria propel themselves. Janine Benyus has written a famous book on this subject entitled 'Biomimicry: Innovation Inspired by Nature'. Biomimicry is learning from organisms or imitating them, in order to solve technical problems.

Benyus observes that man is a relatively young species that can learn from the 30 million survivors that turned earth into a durable ecosystem. She describes many examples that she calls 'a pattern language for survival'. Spiders, bird feathers, trees, anemones: they all provide practical knowledge and inspiration for today's technology developers.

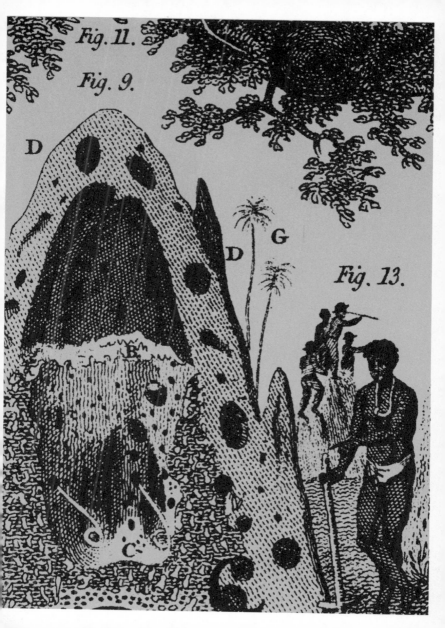

Fig. 11.

Fig. 9.

D

D

G

Fig. 13.

B

C

2.16.
Treemicry

Most people consider nature to consist of everything that lives, apart from themselves. They tend to overlook small but significant details such as mountains, Jupiter and the Universe. Trees are by far the most important representatives of what is considered 'nature'. Perhaps that is why the Barcelona-based architect Enric Ruiz-Geli drew a gigantic stainless steel tree to stand in the middle of the double cone shaped aviary he designed for the Barcelona marine zoo. Wrapped in a net, the metal structure is 62 metres wide at its widest point and 237 metres long to accommodate the birds inside.
The counterfeit tree is not just that. The branches are hollow and at some places there are mats that are moisturized through a system of water pipes. The mats serve as ground for real trees to grow on. The birds can build their nests in them.

project: Cloud 9
architect: Enric Ruiz-Geli
year: 2001
location: Barcelona, Spain

2.17.
Merry manor 1

There is this unavoidable association between the label 'eco' and romantic forest surroundings. For an elderly lady, the French studio Lacaton & Vassal designed a simple minimal dwelling that is almost completely absorbed by the trees around and inside it. The house doesn't even touch the ground and is totally unobtrusive. Interestingly this architecture continuously changes with the seasons. In addition the trees need to be cared for.

project: house in Cap Ferrat
architects: Anne Lacaton,
Jean Philippe Vassal
year: 1998
location: Cap Ferrat, France

2.18.
Merry manor 2

The young architectural practice of
Edouard François and Duncan Lewis
has developed a reputation for this
kind of work in sensitive environmental areas.
In the village of Jupilles, south of Le
Mans, they designed a small community of rental homes for all-year-
round use. To avoid turning the
community into a housing estate each
set of two houses is designed as a box
concealed behind a hedge. In a few
years the 'nature' will completely
cover the houses.

project: rural holiday village, Jupilles
architects: Edouard François with
Duncan Lewis
year: 2000
location: Jupilles, France

2.19.
Green shutters

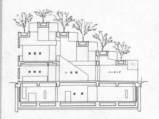

A rule of smart design could be: watch what you're doing. Many houses in New Zealand have a balcony or a veranda on the south side, which is normal from the northern hemisphere's point of view, but in fact rather chilly in summer. Another rule of smart design might be: don't use complex technology unless it is absolutely necessary. Trees are perfectly capable of providing shadow in summer, while allowing the costly light in during winter. This building has a smart slow shutter system consisting of trees. There are of course millions of examples of buildings with the same kind of system, except that in most cases it wasn't designed.

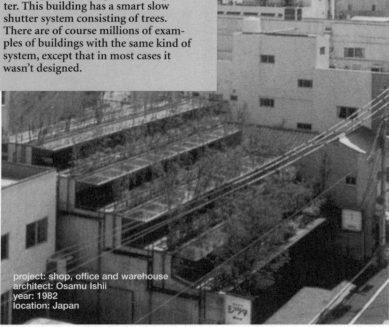

project: shop, office and warehouse
architect: Osamu Ishii
year: 1982
location: Japan

03.
Efficiency
Efficient building

03.
Efficient building

The earth is extremely efficient in maintaining life on and inside its surface. Man on the other hand in his infinite wisdom has wrapped the earth in a somewhat messy layer of extreme inefficiency, to his own disadvantage. For a comparison with man, take his fellow animal the hippopotamus – it is best to use a big creature to make a stronger point. The hippopotamus walks and swims a bit, eats and drinks a lot and excretes the leftovers which are digested and transformed by other fauna and flora. That's it. Man does all that too, but as an extra he has learned to make all kinds of goods to make his life more comfortable: pocket knives, coffee-makers, art, cars, computers, weapons, buildings, ships, cities. Most of these things cannot be digested and their making and transportation and use and disassembly and recycling need energy and landfills. In comparison with the hippopotamus man has made a gigantic leap in consumption, thereby providing the needs and means for even more production and consumption. The richer a nation the more inefficient it is. The easy way out would be to state that man should stop all this. This will never happen because of what we are, but we could try to be more efficient. The first question then is: what is efficient? Most people have an understanding of the word, mainly by comparing observations of simplicity, like the lifestyle of the hippopotamus with their own. Efficiency is an old word and its use probably became more frequent at the beginning of the Industrial Revolution in the mid 19th century. That is when it became a means to define success by producing more with less effort. There are as many definitions of efficiency as there are sciences, but the most economical one is: 'the ratio between what you get and what it costs'. Unfortunately this doesn't really get us anywhere, because there is a whole lot of meaning still missing. 'What you get' doesn't say very much if need and demand are not mentioned. An office building may be what you get, but is there a need for it, or is it a dream come true, or is it a wonderful icon? And is it efficient if only half of it is rented? And is it efficient to replace it after 20 years? Well, it can be. It depends. It is quite impossible to have a general notion of 'what you want'.

The cost is the other part of the incomplete definition. Do we add up design, destruction of wildlife and/or social organization, construction, beauty, enjoyment, location quality, use, networking functionality, exploitation and demolition? Again it depends. Efficiency can be interpreted in many different ways. The main thing that is true in any case is that we have to be careful how we define it and that we have to include as much as is relevant. This holds true for the three main architectural stages: planning and building, use, and disassembly.

Efficiency has always been a major consideration for architecture. Cities owe their very existence to ideas and expectations of efficiency in terms of transportation, trade, weather conditions, geography. Even in the virtual city of Alpha World, building locations are chosen on the basis of simplicity of coordinates, which is efficient, because they take little effort to remember. Cities basically provide a rich environment with short distances between provisions. Interestingly, conditions change with time. A location that was perfect 700 years ago may be a wrong choice in the 21st century. Expanding a city still evolves from considerations of efficiency. It seems more efficient to add new neighbourhoods than to start all over again somewhere else.

Before building starts, many things can be done to take care that appropriate structures will be developed. The first decision to be made is about whether one or more buildings are needed at all at a particular location. Only very few architects dare to propose building nothing at all, or to reuse whatever is already available. Dutch architect Willem Jan Neutelings is an explicit advocate of laziness. He may, for instance, suggest leaving an old building as it is. Some other architects propose that making clothes is sufficient, since keeping warm in them takes a good deal less energy than heating a building. The office of Ken Yeang in Kuala Lumpur is one of the few that make a thorough assessment of the building site, its geological characteristics and the climate at hand. It helps to exploit a location's assets to minimize the need to include climatological appliances. Climate may also influence the structure of a building. The British architect Richard Horden for example, designed a tower that reacts to wind forces by aerodynamically choosing the right position.

Building tradition involves the erection of heavy stony structures that derive their strength and stiffness from resisting pressure forces. Stone bridges from before the Industrial Revolution, before the discovery of iron's ability to resist tensile and bending forces, demonstrate this beautifully. This respectable tradition of sturdily building for eternity, which now embraces concrete for its tremendous applicability in combination with steel, has been the cause of overlooking lighter alternatives. According to lightness specialist Prof Adriaan Beukers, who leads the Laboratory for Lightweight Structures at Delft University of Technology, most buildings could be 50% lighter if not more, by applying different combinations of materials, concepts and processing methods. Currently his laboratory is working on a principle to build high structures that consist of hollow composite shapes filled with air under high pressure, the advantage being that buckling is excluded. The implications of weight reduction are potentially enormous in terms of production and transportation efficiency. Theoretically they would consume a lot less energy if all building components would be, say, 25% lighter. Now it is standard procedure to place concrete piles, chop off the top metre (and in the case of underground building sometimes as much as six metres) and transport these leftovers back to some demolition facility. Even the ancient pyramid builders would have loathed such a procedure. Building sites are usually even more messy than demolition sites. This has its charm for building professionals, but also indicates a lack of efficiency awareness.

The efficiency of lightness may involve replacing material mass with intelligent feedback systems. There have been some experiments in this field. The German pneumatics company Festo has developed pneumatic 'muscles' (tubes that become shorter when the air pressure inside is increased) and their head of development Axel Thallemer led a project to build an inflatable exhibition hall to demonstrate their potential. Of course pneumatic muscles are just one option. Elastic tailoring is another. It involves designing composite structures that change shape in relation to load, a strategy that doesn't require extra energy.

The way buildings are used, however, provides by far the largest contribution to their consumption of effort. They need heating and/or cooling, cleaning and maintenance, and of course water and sewage. These all add up to the cost component of efficiency. In principle there are two strategies to put limitations on this. One could be called 'symbiosis', which involves using the waste of one facility as input to the other, preferably to the benefit of both. The second is self-sufficiency by minimizing input from energy and water systems and output to a sewer system. It is what makes space stations tick, but sophisticated technology is not necessary on earth. Down here it is called autarkic living. Dutch designers and artists are experimenting with it. The two strategies can be combined to further enhance exploitation. If waste water from a home is used to fertilize land on which to grow vegetables, what you get is both autarky and symbiosis at no cost.

Symbiosis is being developed in industry. It is not uncommon to use surplus energy from production to heat buildings. Even tourism is learning to benefit from symbiosis. In a Dutch city called Den Bosch, there is an ice rink situated in the vicinity of an indoor beach. Fake winter heats fake summer. By and large, a lot of heat is still allowed to simply dissipate into the atmosphere. Some people living on the streets have found a way to catch it in the plastic bag they use as a temporary shelter. They just attach the bag to the outlet of a heating system. In this case maybe 'parasite principle' would be a more appropriate name, except that the donor building doesn't really suffer from the extraction of a little warmth.

Autarky is a way to thoroughly integrate a home – but theoretically it could also be an industry – into the ecological cycle at the location where it is built. Studio Schie 2.0 for one is working on ways to make a home entirely independent from all existing piping systems so as to evade the rules these imply. It is designing homes that get their energy from a windmill or solar panels, and from biomass. Their water comes from rain or directly from the photosynthesis process that takes place in trees. Waste water feeds the earth. To experience minimum energy use, the studio closes down all its electrical equipment one day every month. Computer silence frees the thoughts of the people who work there. It is amazing what you can do without electronic devices. Lightness can of course be part of the autarkic principle. If a building doesn't have to be attached to pipes and cables, it doesn't have to be fixed to a place and it doesn't need a heavy foundation. It can drift around on a layer of insulating lightweight foam. The principle of autarky can be extended to the urban scale, like ecosystems. On that level some facilities can be shared, while others are limited to single households.

When the exploitation of a building has reached its end, costs are further increased because it has to be changed, or dismantled or demolished, which may destroy existing value. This should always be weighed against sustaining the existing and reusing parts elsewhere. For many years now recycling is a household word in any kind of production, but sustaining value may increase efficiency in many cases.

Reuse of complete parts has been an important issue for those involved in the idea of 'industrial architecture', but the outcome shows that especially in the realm of building design this is not an easy goal to reach, since every location, and every architect for that matter, requires a different solution. Because of this, production is always limited and expensive. 'Waste mining' is a key notion. It is difficult to set up a system in which architects can search for building parts that 'may come in handy'. Here we find a strong relation with style. On the one hand the architect may have a view on style in which old parts just don't fit. On the other we see that people who bought themselves an old house try to completely return it to its original state. There is a gap in-between that somehow could be filled. A group called 2012 Architects proposes the reuse of components, such as the carcasses of washing machines and submarines, but also buildings and neighbourhoods for purposes other than their original designation. They have brought reuse to a high value level.

Apart from aesthetics reuse is also complex because of the particularities of buildings. They vary in size and they depend on what is available on the site in question. It seems almost impossible to completely exclude the occurrence of 'leftovers'. A way out may be to distinguish in advance between parts that are already available in the waste mine, parts that have to be made new but can be reused later on, and parts that can be recycled or burned, for which someone invented the term 'thermo recycling'. In fact it can even be considered a component of the symbiotic principle if we use the remains of one building to keep another warm. The most interesting issue is the awareness of value: if the costs of creation are high, make sure that the value can be kept up too. This sheds new light on the meaning of efficiency. What you get and what it costs is not a one-shot deal, but rather a ratio that is monitored in time.

3.01.
Evolution of efficiency

Jeroen van den Bergh is a professor in environmental economics at the Free University in Amsterdam. Recently he was awarded the Royal Shell Prize for his research work on sustainable development and energy. Currently his main interest is in evolutionary economics, in which economics is gradually freed from its disciplinary constraints to become analogous to Darwinism. We asked him to help us come to grips with the notion of 'efficiency', since it is very important in relation to the sustainability of city planning and architecture.

It strikes Van den Bergh that the term is so often used in some partial sense. For instance one definition of efficiency is the ratio of work done, by a machine or people, to the cost. 'This to me is a strictly technical approach.

'Economists define efficiency on a social level as well. There it means that no one can be made better off except by the worsening welfare conditions of somebody else.

'In a building a lot of things come together. People like to have a big house, for instance, but it is quite expensive to keep it warm. So where does this leave us with efficiency? Another phenomenon that is always overlooked, when efficiency is defined in the strict technical sense, is the notorious rebound effect.' This is the effect of saving money through efficiency increase. If warming the aforementioned dwelling becomes more efficient and cheaper, the owner may decide that he can afford to fly to Bangkok for a holiday, thereby unknowingly destroying all environmental profit. Efficiency is complex.

We are acquiring more knowledge on the idiosyncrasies of economics, however. Jeroen van den Bergh teaches some basics: 'The first economist Adam Smith believed that if all economic activities were left free this would be to everybody's good. Later on, extra conditions had to be set. There should be no market imperfections and no environmental effects, to name two. Arthur Pigou in the 1920s and '30s was the first to suggest that market failures could be corrected through taxes and subsidies. He came up with the idea of taxing pollution arising from the use of coal and brown coal, the Pigouvian tax. Environmental economics didn't really start until the '60s. Now we know we have to encompass everything, not just profitability which includes environmental costs, but also values like living near water. Efficiency depends on values that not everybody agrees upon. We have to build on hypotheses. Not all parameters can be expressed in numbers. Empirical data has to be complemented with a good policy.

'This implies that design too has to be based on broader ideas. And sometimes you have to take imperfection for granted in the beginning. Sectors with very strict policies can serve as examples. On the whole reuse should be put on a higher level. Waste mining is becoming an important issue. Economists are discussing whether 100% recycling is possible at all.' Ironically

P=WxOxE

The formula describes how we should increase the efficiency (E) in the use of materials and energy to keep the pressure on our environment limited.

On the left there is the pressure on our environment (P), it equals:
W = average global welfare multiplied by
O = the global population multiplied by
E = efficiency

In 1989, when this formula was introduced, the global population was expected to grow four times and its average welfare to grow five times by 2030. To keep the pressure on our environment equal (=1) we should then increase the efficiency (E) in the use of materials and energy by a factor of twenty.

100% recycling is what you get if you calculate on the very long term. Nature doesn't waste a molecule. So we have to find an optimum between short-term efficiency of culture and total absence of waste.

Van den Berg: 'We also have to include use. I mean, there's no simple solution. Ideally we would like to measure everything according to one criterion. More often than not, this is simply money. What people are prepared to pay for a house tells us a lot about their environmental preferences: the amount of greenspace, noise, air pollution, water. Statistics are an important democratic indicator. Money expresses intrinsic value, including religion, ethics and whether frogs are survivors. A lot of data become available if you combine the prices of dwellings with environmental values.

'We have to weigh and aggregate. Economics is similar to ecology. Both study complex systems that are difficult to experiment with. Both deal with flows of energy and recycling. Both need the sun. And both are self-organizing. That's why I consider myself an evolutionary economist. We don't plan as much as we'd like to think.'

3.02.
Eden

The American visionary Richard Buckminster Fuller provided the basic concept for the structure of New Eden, a spectacular public greenhouse in Cornwall. A mid 20th-century master of lightness, Buckminster Fuller invented the principle of tensegrity in which a structure is held up mostly by tensile forces, thereby requiring the least amount of material. We now know that tensegrity is the structural basis for biological organisms all the way from giraffes to one-celled animals. And you can't get more efficient than nature.

His other major proposal is the geodesic dome structure. It consists of a combination of hexagonal frame elements that has been so inspirational that chemists called a peculiar spherical carbon molecule they discovered, with atoms on the corners of hexagons, 'Bucky Balls' or 'Fullerenes'. The Eden roof consists of a snakelike chain of several geodesic domes. Until this building was created, Fuller's domes stood for ambition rather than practice. A number of modest ones had been built, but the idea for a dome to entirely cover Manhattan obviously went a bit too far. The design of domes was always hampered by standard design difficulties: edges and links. A dome must stand on something, needs an entry and may need to be linked to other building elements.

The idea for a structure can be magnificent, but it always has to prove itself in the way it ends and how it relates externally. That is where Eden has improved on earlier solutions. For delivering daylight inside, the obvious solution used to be glass, which is heavy, needs strong, stiff supports and introduces the risk of leakage. Architect Nicholas Grimshaw found an entirely new way to create a translucent dome. It is quite a complex structure of tubes and trusses. The cover is made out of a double layer of antistatic Ethylene Tetra Fluoro Ethylene foil. In each hexagon the double layer is held under pressure with air guided through the tubes to form a cushion. The result is extremely light, certainly in comparison with glass. Making the foil is not very energy intensive. Neither is transportation from the production plant to the building site.

project: New Eden
architect: Nicholas Grimshaw & Partners Ltd.
year: 2001
location: Bodelva, Cornwall, United Kingdom

3.03.
Tall and light

Building technology is gradually developing along the lines of improving and rationalizing traditional methods. Because of the considerable risks involved in high-rise structures due to the concentration of large numbers of people in a very small area, there has not been a major innovative sidestep in tall buildings. They are all basically towers with a steel and concrete structure and glazing to allow in light and containing a comfortable climate. This implies that they are regarded – and this is more important than you would think – as very large houses, while by the sheer number of people inside they can be big enough to be called cities. The logistic effort used in building towers is a principal contributor to the environmental burden. The Sears Tower in Chicago, to name one, weighs about 200,000 tonnes, one fourth of which is steel, enough to produce 50,000 cars. To develop a new type of high-rise structure with minimum environmental impact as far as the building process is concerned, attention could be directed to lightness, thereby reducing the burden caused by material transport, and to replacing the tower concept with the idea of a tall city in which different means and directions of internal transport are possible. The structure could be a city facilitator, an extension of available floor space, rather than a very large house.

At the Laboratory for Lightweight Materials and Structures of the Faculty for Aeronautical Engineering at Delft University of Technology a new principle for very light high-rise building is being developed by Sotiris Koussios and lab head Prof Adriaan Beukers. Basically it can be compared to what it is that allows trees to stand tall in strong winds: the skin dries and loses volume while the core remains moist; because of that the skin is always under tension and less likely to crack through bending forces. The new structure type also features a skin under tension, thereby theoretically excluding the risk of buckling.

The key to required stiffness consists of pressure and smartness. Now let's start with the former. A classic high-rise structure used in Russia for high voltage masts and for a tower in Kobe, Japan in 1940, has recently been proposed for a very tall telecommunications tower. It is held upright with a stay system of steel tension cables placed together as a hyperboloid – call it a cylinder that is narrower in the middle. If this particular structure is made gas tight and filled with air under pressure, the shape will change into an isotensoid, which is any shape wherein, by definition, tensile forces are identical throughout its surface. In this case the shape would be somewhat like that of a rugby ball. It can be defined as one element, several of which can be stacked. It could also be made into one elongated shape, thus turning into a long hose of varying diameter, almost like a caterpillar. If this tube is put under pressure by filling it with a gas or fluid, it will become extremely stiff and theoretically unable to buckle.

The skin is under permanent tension because of the high pressure inside. A tube like that could be made out of fibre reinforced plastic, which is highly resistant to tensile forces, and it could be filled with air. The building process would imply that the hose is put up (or maybe let down from a special lifting airship) and consequently placed under pressure. Columns can be built this way to support floors. Obviously the bottom of a column has to be wider than the top. This implies that the lower floors have less space. A 400-metre-tall, square high-rise with a column at each corner would have some 75% less floor space at the bottom than at the top. The acceptance of loss of floor space determines the limit of height. A range of very light columns of different heights could facilitate a new type of city. Since pressure is easy to measure, built-in intelligence could enhance structure safety.

project: cooling tower of nuclear plant at Schmehausen
engineers: Günter Mayr and Jörg Schlaich
location: Germany
year: 1974

Smart architecture cooperates: it responds to its surroundings. Not only does this apply to the physical environment: climate, urban landscape, conditions like that. It is also true for the social environment, for the political and historical context.

3.04.
Airdrop

You wouldn't expect this kind of inspiring design from a pneumatics company, but Axel Thallemer who leads Corporate Design for Festo in Germany, is something else. His ideas are truly innovative and right on the edge of technology development. Thallemer allows himself to be inspired by what he observes in nature and he succeeds in understanding principles rather than creating banal copies.

In earlier years he designed several mobile buildings. The best known is Airtecture, a rectangular exhibition hall held upright by an inflatable outside skeleton and computer controlled by pneumatic muscles that contract when the air pressure inside them is increased. His most recent design, introduced in 2000, is different altogether. From a distance it looks like a huge drop of water. As a matter of fact this structure, which is 32 metres in diameter and 8 metres high, does involve water. It is inside the foundation ring that keeps the pneumatic structure firmly fixed on the ground without the need for further attachment.

'Airquarium' has a translucent spherical roof made of Vertoflex, a glass fibre reinforced rubber specially developed by Festo and Continental that now has many different applications. The material is harmless when it burns. The whole structure fits into two 20-foot containers, one for the necessary technical equipment and one for the structure consisting of the roof and the ring, of course without the water.

project: Airquarium
research and design:
Axel Thallemer
firm: Festo
year: 2000

3.05.
Water branch

For their project 'Autarkic House' Studio Schie 2.0 built an interesting contraption that literally feeds on natural efficiency. It is a bag that catches tree sweat, or water as we call it. And when you're thirsty you can drink it. Trees 'breathe' carbon dioxide and collect water through their roots to feed the process of photosynthesis by which they produce oxygen in their leaves. As it happens only one per cent of that life-preserving root fluid is actually used. All the rest evaporates, unless of course you catch it in a small zeppelin made out of readily available and cheap PVC electrical tubing and plastic foil.

project: Drinkwaterboom
design: Schie 2.0
year: 2002

3.06. Close to clothes

By far the most efficient means to protect a human being from the weather's whims is clothing. Many people live in conditions that are difficult enough to resort to solutions that can hardly be called buildings anymore. These vary in concept and application. The cities' homeless sometimes use plastic bags that they tie to airconditioning ducts to catch warm air in cold times. Michael Rakowitz designed for them a special 'parasite' bag that feeds on HVAC air and can be used as a warm shelter. They are custom-made. For his first attempt Rakowitz used black bags but this solution was rejected. The homeless prefer visibility over privacy for safety reasons. New York has special regulations. The height of a structure may not exceed a certain limit or it will be considered a tent and therefore illegal. So the designer made it slightly lower. In addition his bag contraptions have been defined as 'body extensions' by court order. So they are viewed as clothes.

'Refuge Wear', designed by Lucy Orta, arose from the observation that entire populations were on the move because of catastrophic circumstances. Several versions of suits that can easily be turned into a tent illustrate her idea of architecture as a body extension, just like Rakowitz's. The system was later updated and called 'Modular

Architecture', which may be too broad a term, but now any number of suits can be linked together to form a collective camp site. Modular Architecture is a way of 'building physical connections between displaced people'.

Iranian born US high-rise architect Nader Khalili travelled through his motherland for five years to discover useful shelter-building methods. He was inspired by ancient mud-brick building in his design for a simple refugee shelter. He makes simple domes with long mud-filled sandbags that are coiled up and held together by barbed wire. The structures are simple enough to be moved from place to place. It is not difficult to combine several into 'superadobes'. Khalili has a vision of entire settlements built from them and even dwellings with three bedrooms and two garages, an entire Broadacre City of mud. NASA has been considering superadobes for putting shelters on the moon. Of course they would replace the barbed wire with Velcro.

(previous page)
product: Parasites
design: Michael Rakowitz
year: 1998

project: Modular Architecture
artist: Lucy Orta
year: 1996

project: Superadobe Domes
design: Nader Khalili
year: 1991

3.07.
Stiff space suit

Fossils require a high quality storage atmosphere if they are to survive even longer than they already have. Temperature variation, for instance, has to be kept within 1°C per year. In regions with unstable climatic conditions this is normally achieved with sophisticated energy-devouring airconditioning machinery. However in the new Natural History Museum in Leiden, Netherlands, the climate control is in the hands of an even more sophisticated system that is far more efficient and cheaper too. For this, architect Fons Verheijen was inspired by space suits.

The floor space of the building is about 25,000 m², half of which contains the priceless fossil collection that originated 180 years ago and which includes the remains of some animals now extinct. The architect decided to put this archive into a tower, to function as a prominent landmark to stimulate development of that particular part of the city. The advantage of a tower is that the climate is easier to control, to the point that some money could be reallocated to the quality of exhibition and office spaces.

The archive cannot be accessed by the public. Bugs that are notorious for damaging fossils cannot travel from floor to floor because the tower is divided up into separate compartments. The clever thing about the tower,

apart from being well insulated, is that the climate control is applied to cavity air inside the walls rather than to the air inside the tower space. The principle is the same in a space suit. It isolates the astronaut from extremely high and low temperatures and underneath the outer layer is an advanced temperature regulation system that preserves the heat generated by the person inside. Superfluous heat is guided through radiators in the astronaut's life pack. Thus the climate of the suit's skin is regulated, not the inside. To protect the tower's interior from rain, the facade has a stainless steel skin on top of a layer of insulating material. Immediately behind that is a 60 millimetre cavity, followed by a 300 millimetre thick layer of concrete. The cavity in-between is divided up into 600 millimetre wide vertical air ducts. Modest equipment at ground level takes care of the airconditioning inside these. The steel outside layer is designed like the scaly skin of a reptile. Shingle overlay absorbs thermal expansion. This tower is an impregnable fortress for temperature changes.

3.08. Steaming briefcase

Energy is not necessarily a big thing, in the literal sense. Building services are becoming smaller and more efficient. In Germany the company Enginion AG is developing an almost zero emission power unit about the size of a briefcase. It is a clean reciprocating engine that drives a pump that compresses water, turning it into steam to drive a dynamo (or some other rotating energy converter) that allows the steam to become water again. It has a host of applications, the same as any power generator.
Fuel cells may speed up the process of 'energy democratization' in the future. A fuel cell is in fact a battery that works on hydrogen. It can be quite small, so small in fact that it could be part of your laptop. Energy efficiency is a matter of time.

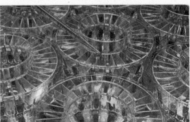

project: archives Naturalis
architect: Fons Verheijen
year: 1997
location: Leiden, the Netherlands

3.09.
Green Building

In the early '90s Future Systems in co-operation with Ove Arup & Partners developed a thorough concept for a Green Building with offices and an up-to-date climate control system. Ideas for a better workplace were integrated with the latest insights on climate control. The entire building is enveloped into a second skin that allows more or less air, light and heat to pass through, depending on the weather conditions outside. The whole structure is set 17 metres above ground level to allow clean air to flow in from underneath. Air is guided through the offices via the central atrium. On the roof is a heat exchange system that collects superfluous energy to warm the incoming air. The building's slick shape is the result of thinking of its enclosure as a second skin. Its principles were soon adopted by many of today's architects.

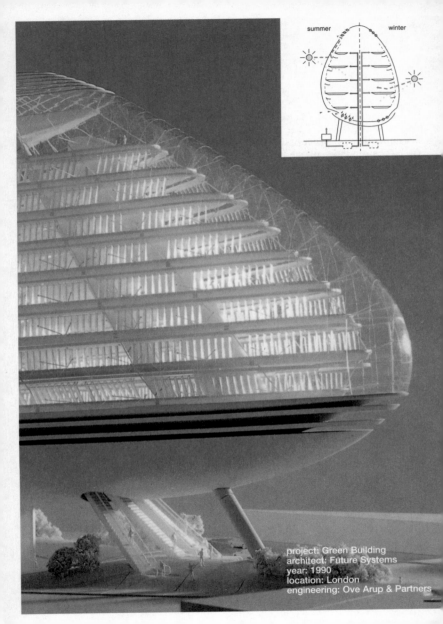

summer   winter

project: Green Building
architect: Future Systems
year: 1990
location: London
engineering: Ove Arup & Partners

3.10.
Efficient styles

Whereas efficient climate control used to be considered peculiar, now it has turned into an asset of prestige. One of the early examples is the main office building for the NMB Bank in Amsterdam by Alberts & Van Huut. It really is a little strange, relating as it does directly to Rudolf Steiner's ideas, with its mountain-like slanted structure, elaborate brickwork and small windows. It is one of those buildings that is loathed by most of the architectural community and loved by the public. Its climatological quality mainly depends on insulation and water flows inside. Alberts & Van Huut continued to refer to organic shapes, but climatic efficiency became subject to modernist architectural conventions about transparency. The NMB Bank is now part of ING Group, an organization with a long history of important architecture commissions. They were one of the early clients of Berlage. Recently Meyer & Van Schooten designed a new high-tech building for their top-level executives in Amsterdam. It features the latest in efficient climate control and bears a strong resemblance to Future Systems' Green Building. To the users inside, the steel structure, glass, gardens and large empty spaces provide a dynamic experience of workspace quality. The look of this slick modern product-form with its aluminium panelling has caused the building to be popularly dubbed 'The Dustbuster'. What remains is the question of whether prestige and efficiency are compatible.

project: ING House
architects: Meyer &
Van Schooten Architecten
year: 2002
location: Amsterdam, the Netherlands

project: Headquarters NMB
architects: Ton Alberts & Max van Huut
year: 1987
location: Amsterdam, the Netherlands

3.11.
UBA Dessau

The German Federal Agency for the Environment can't afford to neglect environmental efficiency. Its new office building is currently under construction and the process is due for completion in 2004. It is being built according to energy consumption standards that are some 50% more strict than those required by law. This noble goal is reached through a combination of intelligent measures. For one thing the building exploits the outside climate to the maximum. When the weather is agreeable the offices have access to natural ventilation. In summer the heat storage capacity of ceilings and walls 'slows down' the temperature changes of day and night. During the day these are nice and cool because of overnight ventilation, and the heat they capture during the day provides warmth in the evenings. Extra heat can be recovered from the thermal mass of the ground, using the largest heat exchangers to date. At least 15% of the energy used by the electrical facilities is supplied by renewable sources. But this is all just technology. The building and its surroundings are expected to provide the sensual feeling of climatic comfort of a park landscape. The building's shape is designed in such a way that a major part of it is accessible to the public. It is entered through the 'UBA Forum' that virtually draws the park inside and serves as a link between public facilities, including a library and a convention hall, and the offices. Even the interior is like a park, featuring islands of greenery. What better way to achieve natural efficiency than to incorporate the natural environment.

project: Umweltbundes Ambt
architect: Sauerbruch Hutton
Architekten, Berlin
year: 2004
location: Dessau, Germany

3.12.
Scooping wind

Ancient wind scoops in Hyderabad, Pakistan, channeling cool afternoon air into each room of the multi-storey housing.

Why is it that design and architecture often involve compensating for the shortcomings of the original plan? Buildings, for instance, are meant to protect people from climatic influences and they end up doing this so well that facilities are required to improve the interior atmosphere. It would be wiser to try and control the impact of weather conditions instead.

Some buildings succeed in doing just that, because they have been designed to turn the wind from outside into a pleasant flow of air inside. It is cheaper, involves less energy and helps avoid the feeling of enclosure you get in an airconditioned space. The principle is very old, and modern examples in Dubai and Hyderabad are derived from it. It is simple too: create a pressure differential between the windward side and the lee side through the clever formation of an obstacle, which is the building itself plus a wind tower that scoops up the air and directs it to the interior.

The wind scooping principle doesn't need a desert climate to function. In Bluewater in the UK Erich Kuhne built an enclosed 'shopping avenue' with an outdoor climate, which is the nicest part of the concept. There is sunshine, no pollution, and fresh air from a natural ventilation system that consists of 12 conical wind scoops able to rotate into the wind.

project: Bluewater shopping centre
architect: Eric Kuhne
engineering: Battle McCarthy
year: 2003
location: Bluewater, United Kingdom

Smart architecture is technology-wise. Using advanced engineering and materials and dressing up a building with energy-saving devices is not necessarily smart, while a distrust of technological solutions is pretty stupid.

3.13.
Sunny clouds

If only the sun would do exactly what we wanted it to: not too much, not too little. This ideal of climatological efficiency has been approached in an academy building in the city of Herne, Germany. The Akademie Mont-Cenis is a glass building with a roof that provides both shadow and energy. With its 12,600 square metres it is the largest roof with an integrated photo voltaic system in the world. It covers a box that contains several buildings: a library, a hotel, a restaurant and the academy complex itself.

Glass structures are notorious for overheating. Shadow is provided by a combination of transparent glass panels and semi-transparent solar panels with six different cell densities. Their carefully engineered arrangement gives the impression of a cloud pattern that allows daylight to enter but also provides pleasantly shaded areas. Palm trees, water and natural ventilation cause the inside climate to be Mediterranean all year through. The inside is estimated to be warmer than the outside only a couple of days a year. But then: no building is perfect.

project: Akademie Mont-Cenis
architects: Jourda &
Perraudin Architectes
year: 1999
location: Herne-Sodingen, Germany

社宅
company housing

コンクリートミキサー
concrete mixer

プラント
plant

オフィス
company office

ミキサー車
mixer truck

駐車場
mixer truck parking

In Tokyo one can play golf in buildings with several floors. Tokyo has to be efficient in its use of space. If it wasn't, there would just be too much going on for this hyper-urban environment to contain. The obvious way to extend the availability of space, and time, is to intelligently and pragmatically combine functions. Atelier Bow-Wow has summarized multiple use of space in this city in a book called 'Made in Tokyo'. It holds many examples of locations that are, for instance, both a department store and an expressway. 'Made in Tokyo' is not about charm, nor about beauty, or function or even construction. All it shows is radically pragmatic use.

The authors define the 'Environmental Unit' as an urban entity characterized by category, structure and use. A department store that is also an expressway, because they share their structure, has more potential for unexpected urban phenomena to occur than a structure that is shared by a department store and, for instance, a restaurant – the same category. On the other hand: if the road and the building at the same location were not even to share their structure, this urban potential would still be enhanced. It is an interesting proposal to understand urban life and, who knows, to make it more efficient.

project: Made in Tokyo
research: Bow-Wow, Momoyo Kaijima, Junzo Kuroda and Yoshiharu Tsukamoto
year: 2001
location: Tokyo, Japan

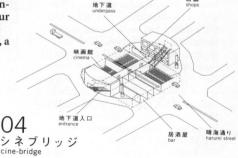

地下道
underpass

店舗
shops

映画館
cinema

地下道入口
entrance

居酒屋
bar

晴海通り
harumi street

04
シネブリッジ
cine-bridge

121

3.15.
Weather
bashing

The main purpose of most buildings is to counteract the capriciousness of weather conditions. Nowadays this is most often done by creating a closed structure with your usual walls and roof and fitting it with electric climate control devices that provide heating when it's cold outside and cooling when it's too damned hot. Generally speaking, this is not a very clever solution, since the structure itself can be designed in such a way that it is capable of providing a comfortable inside climate.

In the 'Jardins de l'imaginaire' in Terrasson, in the middle of an area well-known for the caves of Lascaux and other prehistoric sites, Ian Ritchie built a greenhouse with near-perfect climatic control. It contains a café, a terrace, a shop, an auditorium and an exhibition space. A thick semicircular gabion wall made from crude local stone supports a flat glass roof. The wall is capable of accumulating heat. Because of that, it evens out the temperature change between day and night, a well known principle that has been applied for thousands of years. Between the wall and the roof is a gap which allows air to flow through. In summer this, together with blinds and the air moisturizing effect of plants, keeps the inside cool, something that is difficult to achieve in greenhouses. In addition the ventilation prevents

water from condensing against the glass in spring and autumn. The building is not open to the public in winter, but even then the accumulating wall provides sufficient heating.

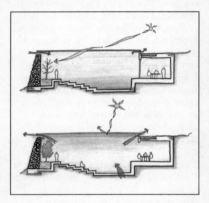

In spring and autumn, the air gap at the edge of the roof prevents condensation. The external wall acts as a heat sink, stabilizing internal temperatures.

In summer, blinds prevent direct sunlight from causing overheating. Evaporation cools the wall, producing 'cold radiation' which improves internal comfort.

project: visitor centre at Terrasson
architect: Ian Ritchie Architects
year: 1995
location: Terrasson, France

3.16.
Broadacre City

Towards the end of his life Frank Lloyd Wright proposed one of the highest skyscrapers ever, but in the 1930s he didn't like the ideas of the International Modern Movement and industrialization at all. He wanted to start a new civilization no less, and he had almost metaphysical notions of what architects could achieve. He wrote: 'A good plan is the beginning and the end, because every good plan is organic. This means that its development in all directions is inherent and unavoidable.' He sought to design the outline of organic urbanization called 'Broadacre City'.

Wright was convinced that all 'Usonian' citizens should be allowed to own land, at least 400 acres of it, to be allocated by a civil architect, thus creating a world in which people could take care of themselves, develop intellectually and do some industrial work on the side. With Broadacre City Wright literally blew up urban life to scatter it across the country. He said: 'It is the country itself, come to life as a truly formidable city.' He was in favour of a radical decentralization based on the opportunities of car travel, which no longer required compactness and even measured prosperity in the number of cars per household. Cultural entertainment was to be provided in community centres and an unfinished cathedral nearby could serve to fulfil people's spiritual needs. Industrial facilities and schools could be made much smaller. Wright was disappointed that America did not accept his Usonian citizenship. His vision of car use turned into a traffic jam reality, but Broadacre City has not entirely lost its inspirational qualities.

project: Broadacre City
architect: Frank Lloyd Wright
year: 1932
location: USA

3.17.
In-betweenness

Landscapes are not always being exploited by official owners. For periods of years they can be in a state of 'in-betweenness', left over from one kind of use and waiting for the next. This does not imply that nobody is interested. People with a keen eye and a feeling for what they need discover these seemingly barren and useless stretches of land and give them a new purpose, albeit temporary. Photographer Bas Princen has turned the observation of people using their particular discovery into a project. Landscapes are pictured in their temporary interpretation by people who like to drive 4x4 cars, spot birds, surf, fly kites, hike or, in this case, build a Millennium Tower.

'Thursday morning, September, future harbour'

3.18.
Urban Lite

The weight of a fire engine holding 30,000 litres of water determines the constructive constraints for roads. Therefore all infrastructure and everything else in the west of the Netherlands for that matter, has to be built on a two-metre layer of sand. This is one of the regulations that determine the quality of reclaimed land. The ground needs to stabilize and lie fallow for a couple of years and all buildings are founded on piles because of that. This procedure interferes with the water balance. Moreover, it costs a fortune to reverse, which renders land exploitation inflexible.

There have been alternative proposals. Wetland, described elsewhere in this book, is one of them. At city scale, MVRDV/Jón Kristinsson have suggested a solution called 'Lite Urbanism' for a location south of Rotterdam. No sand, and the opportunity for a balanced water management using swamps and natural drainage. The infrastructure is a lot simpler too. Telephone cables are gone, as well as gas pipes, as electricity is provided locally by renewable sources on the same level as water purification, which takes place in gardens. Using simple knockdown housing systems, a suburb can be created and disassembled when demands and circumstances change. The concept of the 'light' city can provide a more efficient way of thinking where flexibility, temporariness and even do-it-yourself dwellings are required. And maybe Lite Urbanism can survive with smaller fire engines.

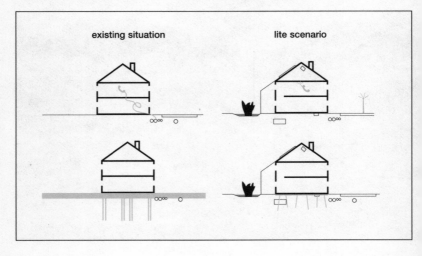

existing situation   lite scenario

04.
Process Practice

left page:
project: Lite Urbanism
architect: MVRDV and Jón Kristinsson
year: 1996
location: Midden-IJsselmonde,
Rotterdam, the Netherlands

04.
Process Practice

Buildings are not inert things, they are alive. This insight seems to be radically altering the way architects work. While many still feel that their buildings look their best on the day they were delivered and ruefully watch their spiritual off-spring age from that day on, more and more are grasping the fact that buildings are not some lifeless end-product but that they change over time. These architects often work at practices where environmental issues are addressed on the road to a sustainable architecture.

If we examine the spectrum of so-called sustainable or eco-logical architecture, we see a 'deep-eco' attitude at one end and a 'high-tech' approach at the other. Both stances locate architecture in time but in fundamentally different ways.
The ideal behind the deep-eco attitude is a cyclic time frame. Just as primitive peoples live in ever recurring cycles of sea-sons and generations, so too should we, for the sake of the en-vironment. The deep-eco attitude rejects progress, seeking instead to at least maintain the status quo from a defensive, conservative position. Instead of the efficiency, momentum and renewal inherent in the process of modernization, it propagates reduction, inactivity and even a return to a pre-in-dustrial era. Buildings designed on the back of this ideal, one might assume, should be fundamentally different from those being built today. In reality, the distinction is not that great. Aside from reinstating many neglected materials and devel-oping eminently usable construction and installation tech-niques, these buildings still look familiar to us.

At the other end of the spectrum is the high-tech attitude whose state-of-the-art application of climate-responsive tech-niques sets out to lessen the building's negative impact on the environment. It slots into the generally accepted time frame, which is linear instead of cyclic. Its practitioners seek to achieve an ideal situation in the future. Everything will be better then, they claim. And if the climate-control equipment doesn't do its job properly, well, just add some more. This strand too has provided many, largely technical innovations. For one thing, innovations in eco-tech have lifted the ban on transparency. Glass buildings were not only notorious energy-wasters, their whole image was negative. High-tech has become eco-tech and has shown during the past decades that energy efficiency and a transparent architecture can go together well.

Much has changed as a result of these developments. In the Netherlands, buildings and urban areas are cleaner and more energy-efficient than they were a few decades ago.
Slowly but surely we have seen energy efficiency, the use of alternative sources of energy and environmentally friendly materials percolating into everyday building and architectural practice. In part through government legislation, in part unquestionably out of a sincere environmental awareness, construction techniques are becoming more enduring, so that the impact of building on the supply of raw materials and fossil fuels is decreasing. But all this has done little to produce a truly new architecture.
Despite these efforts to build a better, cleaner world, current architectural practice can't seem to shake off the traditional image of buildings as static objects and the equally traditional notion of what architects do.

The circumstances surrounding a building's functioning, and accordingly the demands made of it, are constantly altering. This holds for short-term as well as long-term change. The way a building is used can change drastically from one day to the next or even at different times of the day. And it is not only the use that changes, the external circumstances are dynamic too. In the short term, the climate changes in a rhythm of seasons and a rhythm of day and night. In the long term, there is the dynamic of the changing physical and social context. How much more comfortable and enduring buildings would be if they could react flexibly to these changes, if they were to form a self-evident entity with nature! Architects are going to have to reformulate their brief if this is to be achieved.

Instead of being merely the producer of a unique three-dimensional product, architects should see themselves as programmers of a process of spatial change. The time factor and the fact that life is enacted in dynamic processes needs incorporating in the architectural design. A process-based architecture of this order brings about a process rather than a finished article, a set of possibilities that puts the product aspect in the hands of its users. Process-based architects need to concern themselves most of all with creating a field of change and modification, with generating possibilities instead of facts. It doesn't need to be an immaterial, virtual architecture. On the contrary, the presence of a physical, spatial structure always will be a necessary condition for potential use. It is the form that is no longer stable, that is ready to accept change. Its temporary state is determined by the circumstances of the moment on the basis of an activated process and in-built intelligence and potential for change. Not product architecture then, but a process-based architecture whose form is defined by its users' dynamic behaviour and changing demands and by the changing external and internal conditions; an architecture that itself has the characteristics of an ecological system, that emulates nature instead of protecting it and therefore engages in a enduring fusion of nature and culture. Now that would be a truly ground-breaking ecological architecture.

A process-based architecture as described above has yet to become everyday practice. Yet it does exist. In our firm's immediate surroundings we know of several mainly fledgling architectural practices that are working on such a process-targeted approach to architecture, each in their own way. We will be showcasing a number of these neighbouring practices in the final section of the book. Theirs is not the last word on the subject, nor are they the only ones. We are convinced that many such firms exist, maybe still operating in the margin and yet to break surface. Who knows, maybe these are the advance guard of a new, smart, process-oriented architecture.

4.01.
2012
Architecten

2012 architecten;
Jan Jongert, Denis Oudendijk
and Césare Peeren,
Rotterdam.
www.rchitecten.demon.nl

Rottepont, Rotterdam, 2001.
Team: Jan Jongert, Denis
Oudendijk and Césare Peeren.
A building experiment for
'Galerie op de Rotte' by B.E.P..

Witgoedwoning, 1999.
Design by Jan Jongert.
A design and research project
for the Academie van Bouw-
kunst Rotterdam.

Recycle Valley, Beuningen,
2002.
'Van Dirt tot Waste',
a research study into flows of
waste material. Team: Jan
Jongert, Denis Oudendijk and
Césare Peeren. Research in
association with Bureau
Venhuizen.

2012 Architecten is a Rotterdam-based practice run by Jan Jongert, Denis Oudendijk and Césare Peeren. Their basic premise is to address the potential – context, sources of energy, waste materials – at the site where the design is to be realized. Most projects are entirely or partly built by their own workshop. They relate to a variety of scales: graphic design, lighting, furniture, interiors and buildings. A key focus of theirs is to examine how local 'waste' can be recycled as building material. By waste is meant materials and plant as well as empty buildings and urban residual space. Their aim here is to reuse this waste on site with a minimum of additional energy. This is why they established 'Recyclicity', a network organization whose members work together on practical solutions for re-using waste materials in the construction industry, developing new applications for the purpose.

In the context of Recyclicity, the concept of waste has no limitations in scale. Empty buildings and non-used urban space are therefore also considered as waste. The characteristic qualities available at these scales are often neglected or simply ignored. Appliances, refrigerators for example, are being dismantled and stored away or shredded. However, if the waste fridge were to be taken as the starting point, it could lead to an alternative reuse for construction.
Buildings due to be demolished can be considered waste as well. Sometimes whole neighbourhoods are being torn down in order to rebuild so-called environmentally-friendly dwellings in return. By taking the existing buildings as a starting point for designing, the same neighbourhood can be upgraded while saving a lot of energy and material. Unused urban space is often made inaccessible. By

making landscape architects and policy-makers conscious of this waste of space, new uses for it can be stimulated.

Designing and building with locally available waste materials requires an innovative and fundamentally different design approach. Recyclicity stimulates the architect to approach designing from a conceptual duality: the outcome of the design is a result of both the principal's programme and the identity of the available waste. Designing becomes a continuous process influenced by the environment for which the outcome will be an innovative and exciting architectural design – and therefore a far more compatible product than at present.

Rottepont
The 'Rottepont' is one of the first results of Recyclicity. During the summer of 2001, in conjunction with an arts event in Rotterdam, this temporary crossing for pedestrians operated between the banks of the Rotte, the river that gave the city its name. It may not be the most efficient way of crossing a river but certainly the most entertaining and it keeps you fit as well.

The Rottepont is a variant on the traditional pedestrian ferry which is winched or hauled along a cable. The initial sketches brought its designers to the idea of constructing a ferry that used a reel for a winch. A cable manufacturer in the Rotterdam area throws away something like 75 wooden reels of various sizes every month. These reels consist of two large wooden discs separated by a drum of curved staves clamped together with studs – the perfect starting point for a sturdy winch. During the course of the project this winch, built up of five of these wooden reels, ended up as a boat. Walking on the upper reel drives the four lower ones. These four are filled with second-hand car inner tubes and act as floats. During operations the cable attached to the two quays is rolled on and off these reels. Two sets of steps were added to bridge the difference in height between the two quays. They are made from the curved staves of the wooden drums, hence their undulating form.

When the art event was over, the ferry's components were transformed into a 'play object' in Gerard Scholtenstraat in Rotterdam and parts of a work bike in The Hague.

Witgoedwoning

Every year, some 10,000 refrigerators are thrown away in the Rotterdam area. 'Recyclicity Feyenoord', a research project done in 1999, produced a house built using the enormous quantity of discarded fridges and other kitchen appliances. Something like 22 houses could in fact be built every year using this supply of discarded white goods. This 'white goods house' consists of a main loadbearing structure of disused train rails, pairs of fridge sides for insulation (entire fridges on the north side of the house) and a cladding of stainless steel draining boards. Washing machine doors can be mounted as windows in the recesses for kitchen sinks at places chosen by the occupants. As these products are standardized to an extreme, it is a simple matter assembling kits of parts for this house.

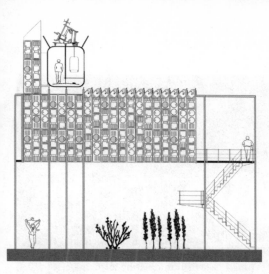

A predecessor of the
Miele space station
(see 1.10.)

Recycle Valley, Beuningen

Near the Dutch town of Beuningen north-west of
Nijmegen, there are enormous sand excavations
afoot for building activities and major infrastructure works, including laying the tracks for the
high-speed railway line to Paris. Interventions like
these transform the site during the course of the
operation into a lunar landscape which could
conceivably be used to house a temporary programme. The departure-point of this project is to
challenge designers with proposals for temporary
programmes, to respect the received context as
much as can be and not to use more materials and
energy flows than are strictly necessary. So 2012
Architecten began by making a material inventory
of all the waste flows in the municipality of Beuningen. The result is a series of product sheets with
descriptions of the origin, material properties and
potential applications of the found waste. These
make a distinction between production waste, recycled materials and materials at the end of a life
cycle. The products and knowledge assembled in
the product sheets enable a great many waste

products to be reused locally as building material –
this way the excavation can become an inventive
Recycle Valley.

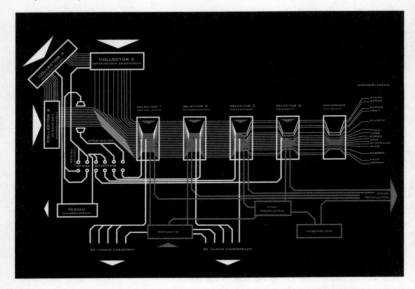

If a building material has lost
its original function, i.e. has
become waste, there is still
plenty you can do with it. The
uppermost flows in the diagram have already been
developed and are working at
maximum efficiency; those
coloured red still have an
enormous untapped potential
open to them.

4.01.
Lofvers van Bergen Kolpa Architecten

Lofvers van Bergen Kolpa Architecten; Willemijn Lofvers, Jago van Bergen and Evert Kolpa, Rotterdam.

Delta-Works, 2003.
Team: Willemijn Lofvers, Jago van Bergen, Evert Kolpa and Loic Fumeaux. Technical advice: Dike Board Rijnland. Design for a competition held by Atelier HSL.

Groen Front!, 2002.
Team: Willemijn Lofvers, Jago van Bergen, Evert Kolpa and Remko Toonen. Design for the competition 'Mix to the Max', held by Bouwfonds Wonen.

IJ-Mast, Amsterdam, 2001.
Team: Willemijn Lofvers, Jago van Bergen, Evert Kolpa and Remko Toonen.
Client: Nozema.

Lofvers van Bergen Kolpa Architecten is an architectural practice based in Rotterdam. Willemijn Lofvers, Jago van Bergen and Evert Kolpa specialize in projects whose focus is a natural balance between programme, landscape and forms of energy, often making inventive use of the seeming contradictions between design brief, technology and context. Their work (designing and realizing buildings, developing scenarios and doing research) runs the gamut of scales. It includes developing sustainable business parks and designing a 150-metre-tall transmitter mast to be built in Amsterdam. Recently they began a three-year research project with students on the future of utilitarian resources – agriculture, energy and water – in the Netherlands.

Delta-Works

The élan of the high-speed rail connection in Europe has a functional as well as a strongly symbolic meaning. It is a very adequate public transport system on a European scale, but also expresses the mental and spatial connection between the different European cultures and types of landscape. The Dutch Delta-HSL will open up the northern flatlands, recognizable from the well-known image of the man-made landscape gained from the water by using wind. The theme of water and wind will be made explicit in the design of the stations, trains and the places left over after planning and construction. One of these, left over after completion of the railway track, will be a huge ground depot in the polderlands of Haarlemmermeer (NL) that facilitates the construction of the Delta-HSL. How can such a place become not just a landmark but

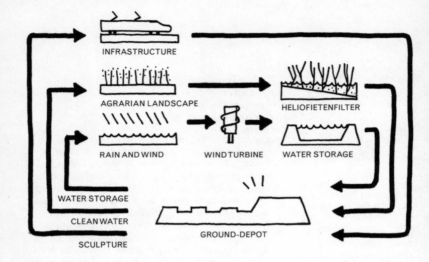

INFRASTRUCTURE

AGRARIAN LANDSCAPE

HELIOFIETENFILTER

RAIN AND WIND

WIND TURBINE

WATER STORAGE

WATER STORAGE

CLEAN WATER

SCULPTURE

GROUND-DEPOT

Ground depot
The soil, mainly clay and peat, will be processed in the body of the dikes. These are sealed off with a layer of clay and overgrown with grass (local vegetation). Both water basin and filter are saved from the soil.

Waterway
The polder is situated at 4.4 metres below sea level. For rainwater to leave the polder it has to be pumped to a higher level. A system of ditches and canals brings the water to the main canal in the middle of the polder. A pumping engine then pumps the water to a higher level and into a subsequent canal (Ringvaart) from where it flows to the sea.

Water storage
In the Haarlemmermeer there is a greater need for expansion basins on a higher level. This way, the stored water will not put pressure on the

also contribute on different levels to its environment?

The famous image of the flat northern lowlands is defined by the continuous struggle against the water. The ingenious hydraulic engineering works of the 19th century made it possible to retrieve land for agricultural production, and created the most important field of production of the Dutch economy. However, intensive harvesting and the mechanical maintenance of the landscape by controlling the water level, has its drawbacks. The soil is exhausted and over-fertilized, the water balance disturbed and the natural environment in the large-scale agrarian areas fragmented, slowly threatening the future of these landscapes and their engineering works.

Besides that, laying out vast infrastructure works like the Delta-HSL disturbs the water balance of the surrounding areas in a dramatic way. Therefore, this project proposes an intervention in the form of this ground depot to restore the natural balance and even contribute to tackling some of the problems relating to the future of the man-made landscape.

Delta-Works is designed as a kinetic sculpture at the juncture of four types of infrastructure. This piece of art is a small-scale hydraulic engineering work set on top of the old soil spill. It purifies water from the polder, at the same time functioning as water storage and generating extra capacity as a pumping engine. Polder water, polluted by agriculture, will be pumped up by an Archimedean screw to the level of the water basin. The basin has enough capacity to function as water storage. Step by step the water will enter the 'helofytenfilters' or reed fields for cleansing. Wind turbines at the site's highest point generate the required energy. Delta-Works is a contemporary self-supporting low-tech water machine at a leftover place.

Groen Front!

Groen Front! (Green front) is a design for a building with a mixed programme of housing, offices and shops. A striking feature is the wide range of strong links it forges in a single complex between the live/work programme and such elements of building performance as climate control and water management. Its location is striking too, being right up against a large natural area, the lakes of Oostvaarderplassen near Almere (NL). The various programmes are strung together in and around the live/work building into a dynamic ecology. Its climatological heart is an odd-shaped lobby which exchanges energy flows between the homes and offices. A series of reed balconies terminating in a spiral serves to purify rain and internal waste water. There are, in addition, basins alongside vegetable gardens in the grounds of the complex, a natural swimming pool warmed by office heat and a sauna under the solar boiler roof. Groen Front! is attractive not just because it places shops and offices near housing but through the strong 'green' identity woven into it. (see illustration on the next page)

ground water and cause seepage.

Pump capacity
Four pumping engines bring the water out of the polder into the Ringvaart. The construction of the Delta-HSL makes extra capacity necessary, due to the fact that the water system is cut into smaller fragments.

Helofytenfilter
Polder water is mainly polluted by nitrogen, phosphorus and pesticide caused by agriculture. Nitrogen and phosphorus can be removed from water by a 'helofytenfilter', a reed landscape in 1.5 metres of water.

Archimedean screw and wind turbine
A wind turbine will drive the Archimedean screw. The Archimedean screw is a proven pumping system, a compound of a propeller shaft with blades. These are placed in an inclined trough, through which the water is propelled upwards.

Construction and maintenance
The raised plateau is easily realized with the available soil and simple ground shifting. The planting requires little maintenance; basic mowing and the yearly reed harvesting are sufficient. The wind turbines and the Archimedean screws are installed and maintained by the dike board.

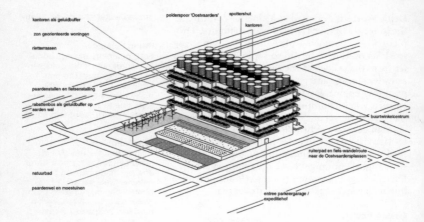

kantoren als geluidbuffer
zon georiënteerde woningen
rietterrassen
paardenstallen en fietsenstalling
rabattenbos als geluidbuffer op aarden wal
natuurbad
paardenwei en moestuinen

polderspoor 'Oostvaarders'
spottershut
kantoren

buurtwinkelcentrum

ruiterpad en fiets-wandelroute naar de Oostvaardersplassen

entree parkeergarage / expeditiehof

Green Front (previous page)

IJ-Mast television transmitter, Amsterdam

This 150-metre-tall television transmitter with natural air-conditioning is being built in the north of Amsterdam for Nozema (the Netherlands Broadcasting Transmission Company). Its aerials sit atop a massive concrete-clad foot with the services integrated into it. The concrete was poured in place using ribbed formwork, giving a measure of aesthetic refinement to the facing. It also has a practical purpose internally. The horizontal ribs use air from outside to cool the cooling water of the transmitting equipment in a natural process. This increases the building's energy efficiency.

The whole is physically articulated to express the programmes and ranges of the various aerials. It also takes account of its visibility from different perspectives and at different times of the day. At night its top will glow like a magic wand in the sky above North Amsterdam.

4.03.
RUIMTELAB

RUIMTELAB; René Heijne and
Jacques Vink, Rotterdam.
www.smartarch.nl/ruimtelab

**Flex buildings, Study into
flexibility**
Team: René Heijne, Jacques Vink
and others.
Client: Rijksplanologische
Dienst and Rijksgebouwen-
dienst. With financial assistance
from the Netherlands Foundation
for the Fine Arts, Design and
Architecture.

F.G. University, Wyong, Australia,
1996 (see 1.02.).

Scouting Club, Reeuwijk near
Gouda, 2001 (design).
Team: René Heijne and
Jacques Vink with Joris
Ghyssaert. Client: Cornelis de
Houtmangroep.

Student housing, Wageningen,
2003.
Team: René Heijne and Jacques
Vink. Client: Stichting Sociale
Huisvesting Wageningen.

Townhouses, Amsterdam, 2000.
Team René Heijne and Jacques
Vink with Guido Duba. Client:
Houtman Radema Family.

Mixed-use building, Hoorn, 2003
(design).
Team: René Heijne and
Jacques Vink with Dieter Dettling.
Client: Municipality of Hoorn.

The RUIMTELAB architectural practice is a
laboratory for flexibility where the architects René
Heijne and Jacques Vink liaise with a network of
experts. Their stepping-off point is that you can
only achieve ground-breaking projects through a
combination of research and design. RUIMTELAB
has carried out studies commissioned by the government into buildings that can be easily modified: flex buildings. It is clear from this research
that it takes more than civil engineering to successfully realize such buildings. Aspects of use and
management are at least as important. Besides, it
requires designers who are willing to let go of their
design. For the result is not a completed 'architectural' product but a continually changing object.
At the time of going to press, RUIMTELAB is
working with an environmental psychologist, an
architectural historian, a structural engineer and a
property consultant on designs for soon-to-be-
built flexible buildings.

Flex buildings are buildings which are literally designed to change. A flex building must be able to
accept different infills and its users must be able to
easily adapt their surroundings. The study into
flex buildings has elicited a number of design insights which are summarized below headed by a
relevant key term. It should be stressed that these
are not hard-and-fast conclusions but more in the
region of statements and reminders for those involved with flex buildings.

1. Flexible is...
Flexibility in a building is its capacity to undergo
modifications and accept changes of function with
limited structural interventions. More than 40%

143

of the activities housed in a flex building can continue to function during modification.

2. An observation
Building regulations are not geared to buildings developed without a pre-established programme. Thinking in terms of function begins with the land use plan.

3. Intensive
Flex buildings enlarge the dynamic of a city by enabling a more intensive land use.

4. Vacancy
A new development is to strategically reserve extra space (oversize) to accommodate future growth, and to accept temporary vacancy to enhance a building's flexibility. Until a few years ago it was customary to avoid leaving buildings vacant because of the bad image. Times change.

5. Nodes
The developments at nodes in the personal transport network are dynamic and difficult to predict. Flex buildings are able to take up these changes.

6. Shrinkage
Building flexibly is not just about growing but also about getting smaller.

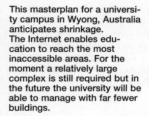

7. Dilemma
Buildings should be able to change quickly to keep abreast of the city's growth. At the same time there

is an urgent need for buildings that act as enduring landmarks in the city. Flex buildings have an answer to this dilemma.

8. Cultural durability
Cultural durability can make a flex building in good working order a major success, but it can also obstruct change, say if there is resistance to demolishing a poorly functioning building.

9. Spontaneous
Sometimes buildings are flexible without this being calculated beforehand. Many warehouses are able to accommodate different kinds of uses through the sturdiness of their architecture.

10. Designing
Many architects (certainly Dutch ones) have been trained along functionalist lines. Functional design assumes buildings with a clearly described programme. In flexible buildings however both the use and the future users are largely unknown.

11. Time horizon
A time horizon is the span of time assumed in a design brief: 20 years means making other decisions than when the horizon is 200 years. It's not just about what a design should do but also for how long.

12. Bandwidth
A flex building need not necessarily be able to take up every possible function. 'Functional bandwidth' is a current term: which functions are involved? You don't always need flexibility.

13. Not everything
The flex building concept suggests an opposite pole: a building made to measure. Not all functions are suitable for inclusion in a flex building. A print-

Farms and stables have also proved suitable for many kinds of use. The modern modular construction used for the agricultural industry seems to have saved the day for a scouting club (Cornelis de Houtmangroep) in Reeuwijk near Gouda. Although it didn't have enough money for a new clubhouse, it did have enough enthusiastic and practically-minded members. So the club commissioned a construction company to erect an inexpensive and roomy stable that its members could fill in themselves.

ing works for instance, with enormous floor loads, is better off with a building made to measure.

This student housing in Wageningen was designed to be able to change in the future. Not everything is possible however. The construction is such as to accept hybrid forms of dwelling and working. But you can't park on the roof!

14. Oversize
By deliberately incorporating excessive space and construction a building has the necessary leeway to accommodate future developments.
A building's flexibility is enhanced by overmeasure in structure as well as space.

15. Facade
The facade design figures prominently in designing flexible buildings. It makes special demands on the design's presentation during the design process, as the building can assume different appearances over time.

In the evening when the lights go on inside, the facade of these twin houses in Amsterdam becomes transparent. During the day, the position of the hatches makes for a changing image.

16. Integration
It can be advantageous financially to integrate and combine layers in a building – such as the construction and the frontage in a loadbearing facade. This can be extremely impracticable however where flexibility is concerned. Necessary changes can lead to the building being demolished prematurely.

17. Compartments
For big buildings erected in stages it is handy to work with compartments. Parts that are finished

combine as a single entity. They can always be recast as individuals at a later date.

18. Double facade
The double facade is a promising concept that allows for expressive and/or open facades in flexible buildings. It can also help to reduce a building's energy consumption.

This mixed-use building in Hoorn sports a double facade. This renders the activities inside the building visible in the exterior. The facade works as a display window in which each of the companies can present itself.

19. Energy
It is sensible to tailor the energy management exactly to the use. So in a flex building the energy management is flexible too.

20. Active management
Flex buildings require active management. Besides the day-to-day business of upkeep and repair, there needs to be a policy for the building's infill. This includes deciding which users and uses are desirable and in which proportions, and fixing the requirements for user representation in the facade.

Visiting the INIT-building in Amsterdam. Students are shown around by RUIMTELAB and project architect Gert de Graaf of Groosman Partners.

4.04.
Schie 2.0

The Rotterdam-based architectural practice Schie 2.0 gives shape to the public realm with commissions that vary between art and urban design. The firm's projects are linked by a conceptual agenda: giving form to the relationships between freedom and responsibility, sustainability and consumerism, and nature and urbanity. In doing so it sets out to answer posed and unposed questions from the perspective of the public realm in a continually changing society. Individualization and globalization have changed the conditions in the public realm so much that there is no longer one but several public domains. It is these that the firm seeks to understand and intensify.

Schie 2.0; Jan Konings, Guido Marsille and Claus Wiersma, Rotterdam.
www.autarkischhuis.nl

IJburg Snack Counter, IJburg, Amsterdam, 1998.
Team: Jan Konings, Ton Matton, Lucas Verweij, Nadja Casabella, Suzanne van Remmen with Hottonia – Vincent Kuypers.
Client: de Architecten Cie, Amsterdam

The Autarkic House, Hoogvliet, Rotterdam 1999.
Team: Jan Konings, Ton Matton, Lucas Verweij, Guido Marsille, Claus Wiersma.
Client: Foundation The Autarkic House.

Seven street-pieces for Almere, Tussen de Vaarten, Almere, 2001.
Team: Jan Konings, Ton Matton, Lucas Verweij, Peter Zoderer, Tonnie van Beek.
Client: De Paviljoens, Almeers Centrum Hedendaagse Kunst, Almere.

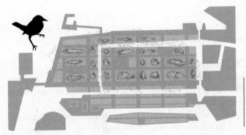

zwarte roodstaart

IJburg Snack Counter
IJburg Snack Counter is a sort of fast-food vending machine for birds. When landscaping Haveneiland (one of the six islands comprising IJburg, a residential area in the making east of Amsterdam) ecological advice based on the bird food pyramid elicited a number of conditions for the design. These in turn produced nine different biotopes attractive to various bird species.
The more complete the structure's composition and variation, the more complete the food chain.

A healthy all-round food chain has predators at the top and the food producers forming the base of the food pyramid. And although it is not a nature reserve, the urban nature of IJburg can become at least as diverse. And in an urban environment of this order it is not just people who ought to benefit from a fast food counter; it can give our feathered friends a welcome meal too.

Autarkic House

This Autarkic House is a self-supporting house whose use of modern-day environmental techniques (notably without wiring, ducting and sewerage) frees it from conventional infrastructure. Aided by wireless networks, the occupant can still stay linked to the world outside. The house has no foundations, is easily dismantled and can be moved around. So it can be placed anywhere, also in extremely low-density areas. A self-supporting house enables a flexible and multifunctional use of space – even in what would normally be utterly uneconomical densities, say one house per hectare.

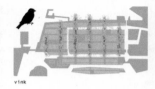

vink

karekiet

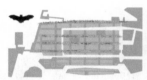

vleermuis

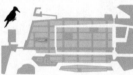

grote bonte specht

The Autarkic House is a prototype that is to be inhabited at three different sites during a nine-year period. The first is on an unfinished stretch of motorway in the Rotterdam area (the A4). The second is a scenic area in the municipality of Lingewaal in Gelderland (NL). The third and last site has an agricultural setting.

Seven street-pieces for Almere

The uniformity of public open space evident in the recent government-designated sites for urban expansion (so-called VINEX districts) is the aftermath of too many conventions, too much fitness for purpose and too much legislation. Streets have become storage cupboards for essential urban components and lack all flexibility. This project for an expansion area in Almere (NL) shows how a street might look if the legislation and use with respect to street layout were to be interpreted differently. The pieces of street become a orchard, a heath, a plaza, a copse; in other words a mature public space with its own dynamic and room for conflict.

4.05.
STEALTHgroup

STEALTHgroup; Ana Dzokic, Marc Neelen, Milica Topalovic and Ivan Kucina, Rotterdam and Belgrade.
www.stealth-g.net

The Wild City
Team: Ana Dzokic, Milica Topalovic, Marc Neelen, Ivan Kucina (STEALTHgroup), with Raoul Bunschoten (Berlage Institute Rotterdam), and students of the Faculty of Architecture, Belgrade.
www.archined.nl/wildcity

3/4 Process + 1/4 Matter
Team: Ana Dzokic, Marc Neelen, Milica Topalovic, Ivan Kucina (STEALTHgroup); Mario Campanella; Ivan Lazarevic (Omnicom), with Fareed Armaly and Milan Cirkovic. With financial assistance from The Daniel Langlois Foundation for Art, Science and Technology (Montreal, Canada) and The Forberg Schneider Foundation (Munich, Germany).
photo credits p. 152: Milan Bozic, Darko Radovanovic.
www.processmatter.net

Amsterdam.North.tmp
Team: Milica Topalovic, Marc Neelen, Ana Dzokic (STEALTHgroup) with Rob Vooren, Con Vleugel and Ted Zwietering (City Administration, Amsterdam North) as part of the EU research programme 'Urban Catalyst'.

STEALTHgroup, a research and design collective based in Rotterdam and Belgrade, originates from the field of architecture and deals with the dynamics of contemporary urban changes. Its projects bring together concepts and expertise from very diverse fields – architecture, urbanism, design, city management, artificial life, software development, media – so as to attune the different approaches. Through experimental work in Belgrade (the Wild City project) the collective has developed ways of observing and registering complex urban phenomena, while in other projects (including Process-Matter) the translation into digital simulation environments has been made. In urban scenarios for Amsterdam (AmsterdamNoord.tmp) STEALTHgroup explores the boundaries of emergent planning within the framework of large-scale urban redevelopments. By crossing different areas of expertise, conceptual fields start amplifying each other – with the aim of developing a feeling for more integrated and adaptive designs and provide a not-taken-for-granted way of looking at the city.

The Wild City >
a laboratory of urban transformation

The project Wild City focuses on developing methodologies for seeing and understanding the forces that change cities nowadays. With the society and urban models of the 'first modernity' fading out and economies changing, the different positions of power structures and of individuals are altering the working of urban systems and their dynamics. The example of Belgrade during the 1990s connects to these large-scale processes. However, it is not a conventional example but a compressed and extreme case; an instance in the fall-off of the collateral events of an evidently changing reality. Against the background of the disintegration of former Yugoslavia and the subsequent UN embargo of 1992, the city of Belgrade faced a gradual erasure of its economy, governmental structures and planning systems. Emergent processes started to replace the city's weakened primary systems in the domains of trade, housing production and public services. What the 'institutions' no longer provided was now compensated by countless individual initiatives using improvisation, ad-hoc interventions and opportunistic solutions. In the resulting reconfiguration of the city tissue many of Belgrade's urban activities became displaced from their initial locations. New urban densities occupied voids, open spaces and infrastructure lines. Nearly every programme, urban type and organization has been altered and tested anew, offering a precise reading of the city's contemporary potentials and needs.

With this growing entropy in the urban environment, the capacities of practices like architecture and planning remain an open question. It is precisely here that this research looks for a different perspective. It started with the assumption that if this seemingly 'chaotic' change to the city can be described and visualized, then ultimately it can become accessible. It is an attempt to track down the immanent logic of change.

To detect and register the changes taking place in Belgrade, a series of random probes along a tramline, cutting through the city from one end to another, were gathered and processed using so-called 'identity cards'. With the next step in the analysis it became possible to describe the character, progression and impact of particular non-regulated processes over time; for instance the way in which wild street commerce overtakes and solidifies in urban public space.

The introduction of the time aspect prompted the idea of creating three-dimensional drawings of both the spatial and the organizational transformation of processes. Information about the development trajectory and the actors is stored (carried) in characteristic time sections. These mappings of time/space phenomena are converted into a set of behaviours that show how in nearly all of the processes, from street trade to city transport, conflict and negotiation between individual actors and institutions give rise to unusual relations and urban typologies. This set of behaviours could be understood as 'urban genes'. Comparing the overall behaviour of all the processes observed brought an exciting discovery: there is a pattern of similarities in behaviour among sequences of 'urban genes'.

3D sequential mapping transformation processes:

Department store
change from trade into management organization that rents its space and shares it with smaller private traders.

Green market
inversion of the space around and at the market by street-sellers.

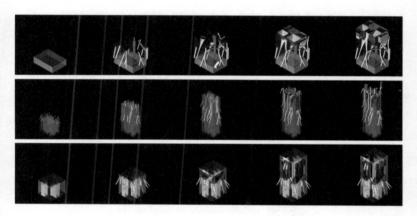

To capture the character and effects of these dynamic systems in the city, comparative studies were made in fields from parallel computing to virology and biology to point out certain characteristics. Generally these systems are flexible, evolvable, resilient, boundless and encourage innovation. Of course, they also have drawbacks by being non-optimal, non-controllable, non-predictable and non-immediate. Seen from a different standpoint, these drawbacks can be read as qualities, too. The city of Belgrade is not a designed masterpiece – it is wild, alive and evolvable and it

Street trade
initiated by selling from boxes and car-hoods, street trade evolved to stands and kiosks. Kiosks became solidified and combining it with housing created a new typology.

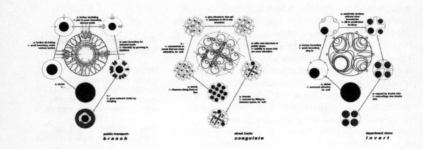

public transport:
branch

street trade:
coagulate

department store:
invert

Through 'urban genes', the mechanics of transformation processes, ranging from street trade to city transport, are extracted. They resemble systems, in which the small elements are in charge of producing newness and flexibility, while the large core maintains the minimum of stability.

shows a surprising agility in exploring opportunities and possibilities.

An integral topic in studying 'urban evolution' concerns urban processes that create or breed innovative outcomes. Belgrade was, for a decade, virtually a laboratory condition open to exploration. The city has acted as an incubator: one that permits and encourages the formation and development of new urban forms, present at all scales and on all levels: spatial, physical, typological, programmatic, organizational... As in the digital evolution model, these 'species' will often supersede a designer's imagination and sharply confront any routine solutions.

3/4 Process + 1/4 Matter > urban processes engineering

Gradually, through different disciplines, an increasing amount of knowledge on the operating of networked environments is becoming available. In architecture, as a result of this, a shift is taking place in the conceptualization of the role played by the designer. The understanding of cities as adaptive and highly interrelated systems poses numerous questions: can architecture (and urban planning) be open to 'spontaneous' innovations? Can it be flexible in interaction with its environment and better equipped as a component of the animate urban network? In response to this, designers and planners might want to formulate more operative attitudes. It would be a move from a top-down, unilateral and project-based architecture toward a more open-ended approach, with emphasis not on singular projects, but on the process of creating environments and on means of steering their course.

Armed with the observations gathered from Belgrade and the Wild City project (where an attempt was made to interpret and describe the city as such a large dispersed system), the sequences of transformations found have been 'ported' to the computational realm, to experiment at the borderline between architecture and simulation software design. A team of architects, an expert in artificial intelligence, an astrophysicist and a group of programmers have begun on this test.

Classic simulation models, like System Dynamics, have for the accuracy of the simulation a system that is as closed as possible and has a good set of statistical data. For urban environments they prove of little value. Urban (and social) systems are rarely closed while the feedback structures can be very subjective. And importantly, they consist of a mix of fairly autonomous elements with on the one hand its individual components and on the other hand the overall planning systems with their own constraints and rules. Thus another approach is needed to translate the adaptation of an urban environment over time.

The knowledge from Belgrade's transformation processes brings in several topics that create input for simulation:
* the multitude of actors – from individual traders and suppliers to city authorities, administration, financial inspection and police;
* the level of control – processes start as 'wild', but in the end reach a balance, as new actors meet institutions 'halfway' to form coalitions;
* the regulation level is dynamic throughout – in observed processes, institutions have not been the initiators of change but were forced to follow

The reconfiguration of public space by the appearance of unregulated street commerce. The diagrams show the local forces that have been identified.

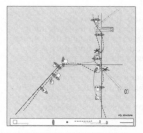

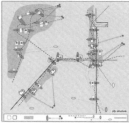

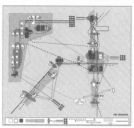

the pace dictated by individual initiatives;
* the level of physical transformation – acting at micro and macro scales (ranging from temporary to solid) with an effect on the total city structure.

This input asked for another approach, Agent-Based Modelling grounded in the local actions of individuals, which in its pure form has scarcely any top-down conventions. Transformed to simulate an urban context, a unique mix of global and local rules is needed to blend the range of variations in control that are crucial in a city.

To what kind of agents can we abstract, for instance, a street trade process? In this case actors (buyers), structures (shops) and a 'controller' (government) and the specific interplay between them are brought into the simulation as the main steering force. Starting from here, a basic simulation tool is then constructed.

When simulation steps are sequenced in time, it is possible to determine the patterns of interaction between the different agents. In this way, their physical and organizational change can be traced, with sensitivity to speed, attraction, strength, success, failure etc.

Of course, it doesn't stop here. The potential role of architects/planners is not only in recognizing and extracting 'spontaneous' urban production, but possibly in influencing, designing and shifting the processes themselves – which means a move of focus from designing objects to designing processes. It enables them to anticipate, involve with and then navigate the possible outcomes within what can be called urban evolutionary design.

Amsterdam.North.tmp >
try-out city
Amsterdam has recently embarked on developing the vast, desolate terrains of the former shipyards on the northern banks of the IJ.

A planning framework has been set up to transform the area over a period of several decades from its industrial function into an urban environment. Not an easy goal for a part of a city that for decades has been considered an urban dump that could absorb unwanted programmes while the city centre developed its cultural and social profile.

'Jump' of urban programmes from central Amsterdam to the North Bank.

In recent years however, the position of Amsterdam North has changed. After various rounds of gentrification during the 1990s, a flood of creative and innovative groups had to leave the city centre and began focusing on the Northern District. Would it be possible to utilize their potential in shaping the transformation of this industrial area? Experience gained from setting up a large-scale cultural hot spot in a derelict wharf building (NDSM Wharf) in the area had already shown a large number of possibilities for unconventional solutions.

In the exploration undertaken, one question became immediately apparent: if the trajectory of the transformation of the Northern IJ embankment takes 25 years, the development doesn't happen at once but in phases (over a territory more than 5 kilometres long); is it then possible to introduce temporary structures and programmes as outposts in the time-space gap of this transition process? Such an approach opens up a new perspective for Amsterdam North, as an urban area that can form a safe shore, an area where ideas, projects and programmes that are too 'fragile' or too 'young' for the commercial competition of the central city will get grounding, time and space to develop in a vivid urban mix. These are people and programmes that take the roughness of the site not as a burden, but consider it rather as an opportunity and source of inspiration. These activities could pioneer the empty lands and premises ahead of the main development process, and by testing the ground indicate possible directions for the future. During the redevelopment process those programmes could weave into the structure of the Masterplan (which regulates the overall spatial development), complementing permanent programmes. Temporary programmes can bridge the gap in use in the development trajectory and respond flexibly to the dynamics of transformation of each specific area/site.

To get a grip on the long-term transformation process, the development of a temporary management plan for the future of the vast dockland area came into focus. It involves the formation of an agency for temporary use. Both are planning tools designed to moderate over time the 'puzzle' of already numerous initiatives and spatial possibilities in the area. A variety of programmes will be sought, in order to allow the area to function as a 'real' city even before all planned structures are implemented.

Planning with temporary uses is very different from regular planning. The major distinction is that it has to be sensitive to very diverse and specific initiatives, generally 'bottom-up', as well as the local dynamics of development at specific sites. Elements of surprise and the unexpected coming from the various proposals are an advantage and a strength of this approach.

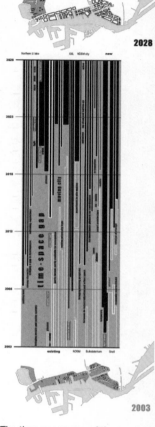

The time-space gap of the development available for temporary use during the 25-year period.

Where next?
Project index
Credits

Where next?

The authors present their personal selection of favourite books and manuals. It is a broad selection, ranging from ecological building, ecological product design and sustainable urbanism to more conceptual approaches to eco-efficiency.

Bioclimatic Architecture
Ken Yeang

Yeang developed his own theory of ecological building, which he named 'bioclimatic architecture'. It includes a thorough understanding of local climate and local building methods. The book explains what bioclimatic architecture is and illustrates the new building typologies and technologies that evolve from Yeang's theory. His buildings combine energy efficiency with improved working and living conditions.
Artemis, London, 1994, ISBN 1-874056-56-0

Biomimicry:
Innovation Inspired By Nature
Janine M. Benyus

Janine Benyus offers us a glimpse of a sustainable future, one in which we imitate or take inspiration from nature's designs and processes to solve human problems.
Among the cases she describes are a solar cell inspired by a leaf and a new agricultural model inspired by the American Prairies. Her book is positive, but not naive. She carefully describes the many obstacles that prevent us from implementing these solutions in the near future.
William Morrow & Company, New York, 1997, ISBN 0-688-16099-9

Cities for a small planet
Richard Rogers

The architect Richard Rogers offers a radical new blueprint for the future of our cities. Only through sustainable planning can we protect the ecology of our planet. Sustainable urban planning is a fundamentally democratic process, involving citizens in decision-making at every level.
Faber and Faber Limited, 1997, ISBN 0-571-17993-2

Design Center Linz
Thomas Herzog

An elaborate description of a truly smart building: the Design Center in Linz by architect Thomas Herzog.
Verlag Gerd Hatje, 1994, ISBN 3-7757 0524-4

Emergence:
The Connected Lives of Ants, Brains, Cities, and Software
Steven Johnson

Makes connections between architecture and urban design and the latest ideas on complex systems and their behaviour.
Penguin Books, London, 2002, ISBN 01-4028-7752

FARMAX
Excursions on density
Winy Maas, Jacob van Rijs with Richard Koek

Projects by MVRDV and studies into urban density, including Lite-Urbanism.
010 Publishers, Rotterdam, 1998, ISBN 90-6450-266-8

Futur Compost (Compound Future):
Design in Barcelona for the next century
Institut de Cultura de Barcelona

Catalogue of a design exhibition entitled 'Futur Compost'. It shows classic exhibits from the mid 1970s onwards, as well as recent conceptual proposals from a handful of young designers, including Martí Guixé's Pharma Food project.
Institut de Cultura de Barcelona, 1999, Spanish/English edition ISBN 84-8156-214-9

Future Systems:
The Story of Tomorrow
Martin Pawley

The architectural consultancy Future Systems, run by Jan Kaplicky and Amanda Levete, is known for its technologically creative design. This can mean transferring modes of construction from the space industry to provide shelters for communities in the developing world or simply selecting materials for their environmentally friendly methods of manufacture. Phaidon Press Limited, London, 1993, ISBN 0-7148-2767-3

The Green Imperative:
Ecology and Ethics in Design and Architecture
Victor Papanek

'There are professions more harmful than industrial design, but only a very few of them', was the opening line of Victor Papanek's classic Design for the Real World, first published in 1970 in Sweden. In essence, The Green Imperative conveys the same message: designers have a moral responsibility to create products that are human in scale, humane, ecologically benign and embedded in social responsibility.
Thames and Hudson Ltd, London, 1995, ISBN 0-500-27846-6

Golden Thread:
2500 Years of Solar Architecture and Technology
Ken Butti and John Perlin

A clear account of the 2500-year history of a technology – solar energy – that many thought was purely a 20th-century development. With beautiful illustrations of historic uses of the sun's energy, and a foreword by Amory Lovins.
Cheshire Books, California, 1980, ISBN 0-917352-08-4

Grow Your Own House:
Simón Vélez and Bamboo Architecture
Alexander von Vegesack and Mateo Kreis (eds)

Bamboo surpasses many a high-tech material. It is lightweight yet exceedingly strong.
This book is about bamboo architecture in general and the work of Simón Vélez in particular. Vélez has been described by some as the 'bamboo Calatrava'.
Vitra Design Museum, Weil am Rhein (BRD), 2000, ISBN 3-931936-25-2

How Buildings Learn:
What happens after they're built
Stewart Brand

Buildings have often been studied wholly in space, but never before have they been studied wholly in time. Stewart Brand proposes that buildings adapt best when constantly refined and reshaped by their occupants, and that architects can mature from being artists of space to becoming artists of time. This book is a rich resource as much for the general reader as for the building professional. It is sure to provoke debate and generate ideas.
Viking Penguin, New York, 1994, ISBN 0-670-83515-3

Keck & Keck
Robert Boyce

The Keck brothers' architectural practice is little known, yet their work is both economically conservative and ecologically conscious. Historian Robert Boyce researched their work and brings to light two long-overlooked but key figures in American architecture.
Princeton Architectural Press, 1993, ISBN 1-878271-17-2

=LANDSCHAP
Dirk Sijmons (ed.)
H+N+S landschapsarchitecten

What Dirk Sijmons thinks about living in the landscape and about area planning, jumps out of all 232 pages of the book =LANDSCHAP that he put together and had published in 1998. A translated selection from the table of contents speaks for itself: 'Green heart? Green metropolis!', 'Rotterdam vacation land' and 'Netherlands is an artwork again'. According to Sijmons nature and culture are a continuation of each other in our country. 'We must stop the eco-rhetoric from the environmental lobby that preaches that being human you can only cause damage.'
Architectura et Natura, Amsterdam, 1998, ISBN 90 71570 81 9 (Dutch only)

Lightness:
The inevitable renaissance of minimum energy structures
Adriaan Beukers and Ed van Hinte

The starting point of the book is that we have to look for novel ways to make things lighter. 'This is simply inevitable, because otherwise the human race will no longer be able to afford mass transportation of goods and people at increasing speeds', according to Ed van Hinte. The book contains numerous examples of light structures and is lavishly illustrated.
010 Publishers, Rotterdam, 1998, ISBN 90-6450-334-6

Low-tech Light-tech High-tech:
Building in the Information Age
Klaus Daniels

The book introduces in theory and practice what sustainable building means in the information age, namely integrated, high-quality, contextual, resource-conserving and efficient building in which ecological assessment and planning are critical. The mechanical engineer Klaus Daniels has produced an impressive, thoroughly researched book.
Birkhäuser Publishers, Basle / Boston / Berlin, 1998, ISBN 0-8176-5861-0

On Growth and Form
D'Arcy Thompson, ed. J.T. Bonner

D'Arcy Thompson was a unique individual – a Greek scholar, a naturalist and a mathematician. He was the first biomathematician. On Growth and Form is a genuine classic on the mathematical and physical aspects of biological form and processes.
Cambridge University Press, Cambridge, 1961(1917), ISBN 0-521-43776-8

Out of Control:
The New Biology of Machines, Social Systems, and the Economic World
Kevin Kelly

Still one of the most inspirational books on complexity, new biology and technology, systems, artificial life and intelligence, and anything related.
Addison-Wesley, Reading, 1994, ISBN 0-201-48340-8

R 128 by Werner Sobek
Werner Blaser and Frank Heinlein

Römerstrasse 128 is an emission-free house which generates its own heating and is fully demountable. In short, a house built with state-of-the-art techniques and eulogized by the architectural press for that and other reasons. 'Already an icon of modern architecture' (Nikolaus Kuhnert in Arch+).
Birkhäuser, Basle, 2001, ISBN 3-7643-6669-9

Rammed Earth / Terra Cruda / Lehm und Architektur
Martin Rauch and Otto Kapfinger

Martin Rauch's great merit is to endow rammed earth construction a place in modern European architecture. Many of the projects he has collaborated on are examples of structures that are not just useful but look great as well.
Birkhäuser, Basle, 2001, ISBN 3-7643-6461-0

Shelter

Written in 1973 and in no time a hippie-architect bible, Shelter gives an inventory of hand-built housing and the building crafts.
Shelter Publications, 1973, ISBN 0-394-70991-8 (paperback)

Smart Design
Ed van Hinte

An inspiring report of the second workshop on Smart Materials and Systems, held at the Netherlands Design Institute from February 28 to March 2, 1998.
Netherlands Design Institute, no ISBN

Sol Power:
The Evolution of Solar Architecture
Sophia and Stefan Behling

The authors of this impressive book show how, from the very earliest forms of constructed dwellings, buildings have been designed to make maximum use of the power of the sun. Sol Power is a READ publication. READ (Renewable Energies in Architecture and Design) is an international group of architects committed to incorporating ecologically sound materials and practices into the architecture of the future.
Prestel, Munich / New York, 1996, ISBN 3-7913-1670-2

Sustainable Architecture
Ed Melet

Regulations aren't a guarantee for sustainable architecture, they can even frustrate new developments. Only by using a broader architectonic language, more experiments and by creating colourful living environments can we arrive at a truly 'green' architecture. Melet presents some thirty projects in the Netherlands and abroad.
NAi Publishers, Rotterdam, 1999, Dutch version ISBN 90-5662-089-4, English version ISBN 90-5662-118-1

Sustainable Architecture and Urbanism: Design, Construction, Examples
Dominique Gauzin-Müller
This book includes descriptions of 26 examples of recent ecological European architecture. Although it sets out to chart the entire European continent it is the German-speaking countries who get most of the attention. Its author has not opted for the showpieces of internationally acclaimed architects for a change. For all that, the chosen examples are of a high architectural quality and inspiring too in that the scale of the buildings and the construction budgets are compatible with current practice among architects.
Birkhäuser, Basle, 2002, ISBN 3-7643-6659-1

The Technology of Ecological Building: Basic Principles and Measures, Examples and Ideas
Klaus Daniels
The book presents the technology needed to integrate the supply of water, heat, cooling, electricity, natural ventilation and lighting into the building's structure and design from the start. Highly recommended reference book.
Birkhäuser Verlag, Basle, 1997, ISBN 3-7643-5461-5

TransPlant: Living Vegetation in Contemporary Art
Barbara Nemitz (ed.)
Explorations of the boundary between nature and culture. The book describes the work of artists for the project 'Künstlergärten' in the Weimar Ilmpark.
Hatje Cantz Verlag, Stuttgart, 2000, ISBN 3-8932-971-X

Trespassers: Inspirations for eco-efficient design
Conny Bakker and Ed van Hinte
This lavishly illustrated volume on eco-efficient design is a compilation of inspiring projects and ideas, four of which were specially done for the book.
010 Publishers, Rotterdam, 1999, ISBN 90-6450-375-3

Vision of the Future
Philips Corporate Design
This book describes the results of a multi-million ECU project carried out by Philips Design which explored life and technology in the near future. Lots of ideas for soft-coloured new products in different 'domains' of life. Most charming from an ecological point of view are the hand-powered products and the solar-powered garments.
V+K Publishing, Bussum (NL), 1996, ISBN 90-66115912

Xtreme Houses
Courtenay Smith and Sean Topham
The cover suggests a book full of computer-generated house designs. Happily that is not the case. Many of the houses have nothing to do with either computers or architects. They were largely built by DIYers, artists, developed by industrial designers or created out of sheer necessity.
Prestel Verlag, Munich, 2002, ISBN 3-7913-2789-5

Your Private Sky:
Buckminster Fuller, the Art of Design Science
Joachim Krausse, Claude Lichtenstein
Your Private Sky has only just been published, but this book, which lovingly describes the life and work of Buckminster Fuller is already a classic. Not to be missed!
Lars Müller Publishers / Birkhäuser Verlag, 1999, ISBN 3-907044-88-6

Project index

1.14.
product:
AlphaWorld
source:
www.activeworlds.com

1.15.
project 1:
Heliport, Hanku
Chayamachi Building,
Osaka, Japan
source:
Aardbevingsbestendig
Bouwen (2), Cement nr. 8-
2000, www.salvado-
ri.org/aoc/9b.html
project 2:
'Seirei' Worship and
Visitors Hall
architect:
Shin Takamatsu Architect &
Associates
year:
1998
location:
Mount Myoken, Nose, Japan
source:
Prof. Ir. F. van Herwijnen
photo credits:
F. van Herwijnen

1.16.
project:
Design Center Linz
architect:
Herzog + Partner,
Architecten BDA, München
year:
1993
location:
Linz, Austria
lighting:
Christian Bartenbach
source:
www.herzog-und-partner.de
photo credits:
Peter Bartenbach

2.01.
image credits:
'Stanford Torus' 1975. From
Richard D. Johnson and
Charles Holbrow, eds.,
Space Settlements:
A Design Study, 1977.

project:
Bios 1, 2 and 3
source:
www.aibs.org/bioscienceli-
brary/vol47/oct97.salis-
bury.text.html
Frank B. Salisbury, Josef I.
Gitelson, and Genry M.
Lisovsky in BioScience,
Volume 47, Number 9
October 1997

2.02.
project:
Biosphere 2 and 3
source:
www.bio2.edu/
www.desertusa.com/
mag99/apr/stories/bi
os2.html

2.03.
product:
EcoSphere®
source:
www.eco-sphere.com

2.04.
project:
Infra-Ecologie
research and design:
Willemijn Lofvers, Jago van
Bergen and Duzan Doepel
year:
1999
location:
the Netherlands

2.05.
source:
www.indigo-
dev.com/Kal.htm2.06.

2.06.
project:
Wetland
architects:
Tom Mossel, Esther
Gonzalez Aurignac with
Bert Fraza
year:
2000
location:
the Netherlands

2.07.
project:
R 128
architect and engineer:
Werner Sobek
year:
2000
location:
Stuttgart, Germany
photo credits:
Roland Halbe

2.08.
project:
Federation Square Labyrinth
and Atrium
architects:
Lab Architecture Studio in
association with Bates Smart
design architects:
Donald L. Bates and Peter
Davidson
environmental engineers:
Atelier Ten
year:
2000
location:
Melbourne, Australia
photo credits:
Mark Roper
source:
www.labarchitecture.com

2.09.
project:
Mewah Oils Headquarters
architects:
T.R. Hamzah & Yeang Sdn.
year:
2003
location:
Port Klang, Selangor,
Malaysia
photo credits:
T.R. Hamzah & Yeang

2.10.
project:
City Fruitful
architects:
Kuiper Compagnons, Kas
Oosterhuis Architekten et al.
year:
1992

location:
Dordrecht, the Netherlands
source:
City Fruitful, 010 Publishers,
Rotterdam, 1992
photo credits:
Kas Oosterhuis Architekten

2.11.
diagram:
The Three Magnets
architect:
Ebenezer Howard
year:
1898
source:
'De ideale stad',
Ruth Eaton p. 147

2.12.
landscape architect:
Dirk Sijmons, H+N+S
Landschapsarchitecten,
Amsterdam
year:
(project) 2003,
proposed for 2005-2020
location:
Kamerik, Randstad,
the Netherlands

2.13.
researcher:
Julian Vincent, Centre for
Biomimetics at the University
of Reading
source:
Encyclopaedia Brittanica
Yearbook of Science and
the Future: Borrowing the
best from nature, 1995

2.14.
project:
Feral Robotic Dog
artist:
Natalie Jeremijenko
product:
fake Aibo (Sony)
firm:
unknown (Made in China)

2.15.
source:
Janine M. Benyus:
Biomimicry, New York, 1997

2.16.
project:
Cloud 9
architect:
Enric Ruiz-Geli
year:
2001
location:
Barcelona, Spain
source:
www.e-cloud9.com
photo credits:
Enric Ruiz-Geli

2.17.
project:
house in Cap Ferrat
architect:
Anne Lacaton,
Jean Philippe Vassal
year:
1998
location:
Cap Ferrat, France
photo credits:
Philippe Ruault

2.18.
project:
rural holiday village, Jupilles
architects:
Edouard Francois &
associès with Duncan Lewis
year:
2000
location:
Jupilles, France
photo credits:
Edouard Francois & associès

2.19.
project:
shop, office and warehouse
architect:
Osamu Ishii, Biken Architectural Design Office
year:
1982
location:
Okayama, Japan

photo credits:
Process Architecture, Plea,

3.01.
researcher:
Jeroen van den Bergh, Free
University in Amsterdam
source formula:
RMNO, Meerjarenvisie
1992; Programma van mi-
lieu- en natuuronderzoek
ten behoeve van een duur-
zame ontwikkeling, RMNO
publication nr.70, 1992
www.shell.com

3.02.
project:
New Eden
architect:
Nicholas Grimshaw &
Partners Ltd.
year:
2001
location:
Bodelva, Cornwall,
United Kingdom
photo credits:
Vector Special Projects Ltd

3.03.
project:
cooling tower, nuclear plant
at Schmehausen
engineering
Günter Mayr, Jörg Schlaich
location:
Germany
photo credits:
l'art de l'ingenieur

3.04.
project:
Airquarium
research and design:
Axel Thallemer
firm:
Festo
year:
2000
source:
www.festo.com/
pneumatic_structures
photo credits:
Festo AG & Co. KG

3.05.
product:
Drinkwaterboom
design:
Schie 2.0, Jan Konings,
Claus Wiersma, Guido
Masille and Joost van Alfen.
year:
2002
photo credits:
Schie 2.0

3.06.
product 1:
Parasites
design:
Michael Rakowitz
year:
1998
source:
www.possibleuto-
pia.com/mike
project 2:
Modular Architecture
artist:
Lucy Orta
year:
1996
source:
www.studio-orta.com
photo credits:
Galerie Anne de Villepoix
project 3:
Superadobe Domes
design:
Nader Khalili
year:
1991
source:
www.callearth.org

3.07.
project:
archives of the Natural
History Museum Naturalis
architect:
Fons Verheijen,
VVKH architecten
engineering:
Technical Management
year:
1997
location:
Leiden, the Netherlands

source:
'Fossielen in een astronau-
tenpak', Architectuur &
Bouwen no. 5, 1997.

3.08.
product:
EZEE
(Equal Zero Emission Engine)
firm:
Enginion AG, Berlin
source:
www.enginion.com

3.09.
project:
Green Building
architect:
Future Systems
year:
1990
location:
London
engineering:
Ove Arup & Partners
source:
www.future-systems.com
Martin Pawley, Future Systems, London, 1993
photo credits:
Richard Davies

3.10.
project 1:
ING House
architects:
Meyer en van Schooten Ar-
chitecten
year:
2002
location:
Amsterdam, the Netherlands
source:
www.meyer-vanschooten.nl
photocredits:
Ruimtelab
project 2:
Headquarters NMB
architects:
Ton Alberts & Max van Huut
year:
1987
location:
Amsterdam, the Netherlands

photo credits:
Alberts & van Huut bv.

3.11.
project:
Umweltbundes Ambt
architect:
Sauerbruch Hutton
Architekten, Berlin
year:
2004
location:
Dessau, Germany

3.12.
project:
Bluewater shopping centre
architect:
Eric Kuhne
engineering:
Battle McCarthy
year:
2003
location:
Bluewater, Kent, United
Kingdom

3.13.
project:
Akademie Mont-Cenis
architects:
Jourda & Perraudin
Architectes
year:
1999
location:
Herne-Sodingen, Germany
photo credits:
Jourda Architectes

3.14.
project:
Made in Tokyo
research:
Bow-Wow, Momoyo
Kaijima, Junzo Kuroda and
Yoshiharu Tsukamoto
year:
2001
location:
Tokyo, Japan
source:
Made in Tokyo, 2001, Tokyo

3.15.
project:
visitor centre at Terrasson
architect:
Ian Ritchie Architects
year:
1995
location:
Terrasson, France
engineers:
Ove Arup & Partners
landscape design:
Kathryn Gustafson,
Paysage Land
photo credits:
Ian Ritchie Architects

3.16.
project:
Broadacre City
architect:
Frank Lloyd Wright
year:
1932
location:
USA
photo credits:
Arizona State University,
College of Architecture and
Environmental Design,
lent by the Frank Lloyd
Wright Foundation

3.17.
photographer:
Bas Princen
year:
2003
location:
the Netherlands

3.18.
project:
Lite Urbanism
architect:
MVRDV and Jón Kristinsson
year:
1996
location:
VINEX site Midden-IJssel-
monde Rotterdam,
the Netherlands
source:
FARMAX, 1998, Rotterdam

project
cover and inserts
photographer:
Paulien Bremmer
location:
underground shelters in
Amsterdam, the Netherlands.
year:
2003

Credits

Smart Architecture was created in close cooperation between Ed van Hinte, Jacques Vink, Marc Neelen, Piet Vollaard and Erik Wong.
Ed van Hinte is a freelance publicist who publishes mainly on design. Erik Wong is a graphic designer. Jacques Vink is an architect and co-founder of the Smart Architecture Foundation, like fellow architect and ArchiNed director Piet Vollaard. Marc Neelen is an architect and a member of the Foundation since its inception.

This book has been made possible by: the Netherlands Architecture Fund and Foundation Prins Bernhard Cultuurfonds

Copy editor: John Kirkpatrick
Printed by: Snoeck-Ducaju & zoon, Ghent

© 2003 The authors and 010 Publishers, Rotterdam (www.010publishers.nl)

ISBN 90 6450 490 3

About the Smart Architecture Foundation:

The mission of Stichting SL.A. is to create and discuss concepts and ideas for buildings and cities that combine optimum performance with a minimal use of materials and energy.
Many of the so-called 'green architects' tend to look upon nature as a victim brutalized by the fierce attacks from 'unnatural' technology. Others look upon environmental issues as a nuisance, a complicating factor in the design process. Stichting SL.A. rejects both views. It is their belief that nature and technology should be looked upon as allies, not enemies or victims. Thus, truly sustainable, integral, SMART solutions can only be found by rethinking the starting points, concepts and typologies of architecture and city planning itself. Stichting SL.A. searches for powerful, green, smart ideas that deliver the much needed innovations in architecture, design and urbanism.

Jacques Vink and Piet Vollaard are the co-founders of Stichting SL.A. (SLimme Architectuur = Smart Architecture). They built www.smartarch.nl with Marc Neelen, Yvo Zijlstra, Marcel van der Zwet and Conny Bakker. Many others contributed with ideas and publications.

Thanks to Machiel van Dorst as guiding spirit of the Foundation. Also to Thomas Linders, Jelle Zijlstra and Albert van Dorssen for chairing the Foundation.